Elementary

Forge Practice

A Text-Book
For Technical and Vocational Schools

BY

ROBERT H. HARCOURT

Instructor in Forge Practice,
Leland Stanford Junior University

Stanford University, Cal.
STANFORD UNIVERSITY PRESS
1917

Elementary Forge Practice

by Robert H. Harcourt

Originally published by
Stanford University Press
Stanford University
California

Original copyright 1917
by Robert H. Harcourt

Reprinted by
Lindsay Publications Inc
Bradley IL 60915

ISBN 1-55918-169-9

1995

4   5   6   7   8   9   0

WARNING

For a fascinating selection of the highest quality books for experimenters, inventors, tinkerers, mad scientists, and a very few normal people... visit
www.lindsaybks.com

PREFACE

The purpose in this book is to give the student of forge practice an understanding of fundamental operations employed, it being realized that many applications of these operations can be learned only thru connection with commercial work.

To this end a series of exercises has been arranged. It is not intended that a student be required to make all of them, but there are certain ones which must be mastered before he can make some of those that follow. They are arranged with the intention of meeting the demands of all classes of students.

Instruction should be given on the first few exercises and on those parts of the more difficult ones which may be hard for the student to understand. The writer has found that in most cases a student can make the simpler exercises with very little instruction if given a drawing showing the different steps to be taken.

The subject matter contained herein has been used at Leland Stanford Junior University for a number of years as a syllabus, together with a set of forgings showing the actual steps. Its use has clearly demonstrated the following advantages.

1. Taking of notes during a lecture is partially elimated, so that a student has the fullest opportunity for watching the entire demonstration. The text is a ready reference in case he does not remember a demonstrated point.

2. Students are able to proceed with the exercises without much instruction, thus saving time.

3. Students make the exercises better and in a shorter period of time.

4. The initiative of the student as well as his ability to work from drawings is developed.

Many thanks are due to Professor E. P. Lesley of Leland Stanford Junior University for his assistance in reading the manuscript; to Mr. W. L. Rifenberick for his work on the preliminary syllabus; and to Mr. H. P. Miller, Jr., for his valuable suggestions and assistance in the preparation of the drawings.

R. H. HARCOURT.

STANFORD UNIVERSITY, May 1917.

CONTENTS

EXERCISES

WARNING

Remember that the materials and methods described here are from another era. Workers were less safety conscious then, and some methods may be downright dangerous. Be careful! Use good solid judgement in your work, and think ahead. Lindsay Publications Inc. has not tested these methods and materials and does not endorse them. Our job is merely to pass along to you information from another era. Safety is your responsibility.

Write for a complete catalog of unusual books available from:

Lindsay Publications Inc
PO Box 12
Bradley IL 60915-0012

Elementary Forge Practice

CHAPTER I

MATERIALS AND EQUIPMENT.

The **Materials** most commonly used in forging are: wrought iron, Norway iron, machine steel, tool steel, and high-speed steel. Their main constituent is iron, as obtained from iron ore; but they differ in the amount of carbon and other elements that are mixed or alloyed with the iron.

Wrought Iron is made by the Puddling Process, and differs from other kinds of iron mainly because of the slag seams introduced during its manufacture. These seams cause the stringy, fibrous appearance of the iron when it is broken or cut cold. They are helpful when welding, since the slag acts as a flux; but they also weaken the iron, and make it liable to crack. Wrought iron is much easier to weld than machine steel, because the range of temperature thru which it may be heated without injury is much greater. It may not be hardened to any appreciable extent. If hammered too much when cold it will burst thru the slag seams.

The percentage of carbon in common wrought iron is very low, being about .04%.

Norway, or Swedish Iron, as imported from Norway and Sweden, is made in a charcoal furnace. It is the purest soft iron on the market, as the ore from which it is made is practically free from phosphorus and sulphur. It is used mainly for intricate work involving much bending and, since it rusts very slowly, for forgings that are exposed to the weather. The best grades of crucible steel produced in this country are also made from this kind of iron.

Machinery Steel, also known as machine steel, low-carbon steel, and mild steel, contains from about .05% to .5% of carbon, and is made by the Open-Hearth or Bessemer Process. It may be easily welded with the aid of a flux, and can be welded without one. Being stronger, more homogeneous and cheaper than wrought iron, it is well adapted for forgings. It cannot be hardened to any very great extent. A piece of good grade $\frac{3}{4}$-inch thick may be bent cold 180° flat on itself without rupture. In general it is found that increasing the carbon content will increase the strength, elasticity and hardening quality, and decrease the ductility and weldability.

This grade of steel differs from wrought iron in that it does not become soft and plastic at the welding heat. It burns or wastes away at a lower temperature than wrought iron, making it more difficult to weld. The crystalline, or granular, appearance of the fracture, the absence of slag seams, and the emery-wheel test described later, are used to distinguish it from wrought iron.

High-Carbon Steel, or tool steel, the best grades of which are made by the Crucible Process, contains carbon in amounts varying from .5% to 1.6%. Steel with a higher carbon content is seldom used. High-carbon steel is generally distinguished from low-carbon steel by the fact that it becomes very hard when heated to a red heat and suddenly cooled. It snaps off when cut cold, on account of the hardness of the ordinary commercial stock. As with mild, or low-carbon steel, the hardening quality varies directly with the carbon content. There are, however, some brands of steel containing less than .5% carbon which harden considerably when heated and cooled quickly; so there is no well marked division between the two classes. High-carbon steel is most difficult to weld.

High-Speed Steel is of special importance in the machine shop on account of its red hardness, or property of retaining a cutting edge at a visible red heat. Tools made from ordinary high-carbon steel, if heated by friction or otherwise to a temperature of about 400° F., begin to lose their hardness; while high-speed steel tools may be heated up to about 1200° F. before they break down from softening.

This property is due to the presence in the steel of from 13% to 19% tungsten. Other elements are present in approximately the percentages given:

Tungsten	Chromium	Carbon	Manganese	Vanadium	Silicon
16.87	2.99	0.65	0.31	0.85	0.27

The Emery-Wheel Test.—The most satisfactory shop method for distinguishing between the different kinds and grades of iron and steel consists in observing the sparks given off when a bar of the material is brought in contact with a rapidly revolving emery-wheel. In general it is found that the more carbon there is present the brighter the sparks will be.

Sparks obtained from wrought iron are light-straw color, and follow straight lines. Machine steel gives off sparks that are much the same in character except that they explode, or fork, to some extent. White sparks which explode much more frequently are obtained from high-carbon steel. Those given off by high-speed steel follow straight lines, similarly to sparks from wrought iron, but give off much less light, and end abruptly in a chrome-yellow, pear-shaped flame.

Weight of Iron.—It is often necessary to know the weight of material used in an iron or steel forging. This can be computed if it is remembered that a cubic foot of steel weighs about 490 pounds, or that a 1-inch square bar 1 foot long weighs 3.40 pounds and a 1-inch round bar of the same length weighs 2.67 pounds.

Shrinkage.—When iron or steel is heated, it expands in direct proportion to the change in temperature. A bar heated to a good forging heat will have each of its linear dimensions increased about ⅛ inch to the foot. Upon cooling it will contract about the same amount.

Bibliography.—For a complete description of the various processes employed in making iron and steel, the student is referred to the following books:

Stoughton: *The Metallurgy of Iron and Steel.* Hill Publishing Co., New York.

Metcalf: *Steel.* John Wiley & Sons, New York.

Forge.—One of the commonest types of forge used in universities and technical schools is shown in Fig. 1. It consists of a cast-iron hearth (*A*) mounted on a suitable base (*H*) and having at its center a fire-pot (*B*). This fire-pot is made in various shapes and sizes, and is sometimes lined with fire-brick. At the bottom of the fire-pot is an opening,

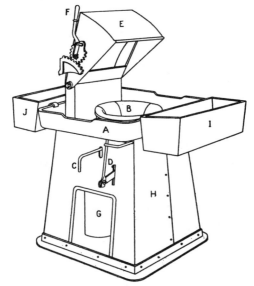

Fig. 1. THE FORGE.

A, hearth; *B*, fire-pot; *C*, tuyere lever; *D*, blast-gate lever; *E*, adjustable hood; *F*, adjusting lever; *G*, exhaust pipe; *H*, base; *I*, coal-box; *J*, coke-box.

called the *tuyere*, thru which the blast is forced. Tuyeres are constructed so as to admit the air readily and at the same time prevent coal from dropping thru them. Some are arranged so that the coal and ashes which do drop thru can be shaken out by means of the tuyere lever (C). The air blast is controlled by means of the blast-gate lever (D).

The forge shown is of the down-draft type, the smoke and gases from the fire being drawn under the adjustable hood (E) and down thru the exhaust pipe (G). The position of the hood can be changed by means of the adjusting lever (F). The boxes (I) and (J) should be used for holding coal and coke respectively, a separate tank for water being advisable.

In commercial shops the forges are generally circular and made of light sheet-steel.

Fire Tools.—The tools required at each forge in order to take proper care of the fire are: coal shovel, fire rake, dipper, and poker.

Coal.—The best "blacksmith's" coal for use in a forge is a high grade of soft or bituminous coal. It can in general be distinguished by the crumbling of the lumps when hit with a hammer; but the most reliable test is to note its characteristics in actual use. When dampened and put on a fire it should cake up, forming good coke and leaving very little clinker when burned. Ordinary soft coal, or steam-coal, makes a very dirty fire, giving off much smoke and leaving a great deal of clinker. It is very disagreeable to work with, on account both of the smoke and of the hot gases given off.

Coal containing either sulphur or phosphorus is to be avoided, as these elements are absorbed by the iron. Sulphur makes the iron hot-short, *i. e.,* brittle while hot; and phosphorus makes it cold-short, or brittle when cold.

Building Fire.—The success of welding and forging depends, to a large extent, on the building and care of the fire. When a fresh fire is to be built, make a hole about 8 inches in diameter at the center of the hearth, removing enough of the dirt and ashes to expose the tuyere. Place some shavings in this hole and on top of them some small lumps of coke. After lighting the shavings, turn the blast on a little and wait until the coke has become red hot. More coke should then be added, forming a cone, and the space around it banked, or filled in, with moist coal. Care must be taken in dampening the coal not to get it too wet, or the water will seep out and run over the tuyere, thereby spoiling the fire. When enough coal has been placed around the fire, it should be leveled off and packed down hard with the back of a shovel. This is done to prevent the air-blast from coming thru at the outer edges of the fire, spreading it over too large an area.

Coke.—It is found that packing also helps materially in the production of coke, which is formed by the caking of the coal after the fire has burned for some time. Coke should be saved when cleaning out the fire or hearth at the end of a period, or when building a second fire. The center of the fire burns out somewhat like a crater, and has to be constantly refilled with extra coke. If it is necessary to have a small fire, the coke should be broken into small pieces.

Making Coke.—When extra coke is required, it can be made by placing some large lumps, of wet coal on top of the fire and allowing it to burn slowly for some time. It should not be disturbed with a poker until it has caked well.

Caution.—Do not continually poke or disturb the fire, but keep the center full of small pieces of coke.

Clinker.—Dirt and dross in the coal form clinker directly above the tuyere. This is a detriment when welding, since it prevents air from coming thru the tuyere and causes a deposit of dirt on the pieces in the fire. For this reason the fire should be cleaned out every half-hour, when welding, by removing the clinker with a poker. Care must be taken to prevent lead and babbitt metal from getting into the fire, as they oxidize and prevent welding.

Banking Fire.—By placing a piece of wood on end in the fire and covering it with coke and coal, the fire will last for some time without air-blast.

Cleaning Fire at End of Period.—When the fire is no longer needed, the coal should be removed and placed in the coal-tank. The coke should then be loosened with the poker, moistened with water, and placed in the coke-tank. The clinker and ashes are dug out and thrown into the ash-box. The forge is then clean and ready for future use.

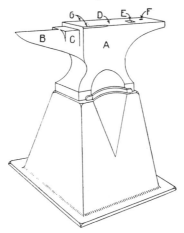

Fig. 2. THE ANVIL.

A, body; *B,* horn; *C,* base of horn; *D,* face; *E,* hardie hole; *F,* pritchel hole; *G,* rounded edges.

Anvil.—The type of anvil generally used is shown in Fig. 2. The body (*A*) is usually made of wrought iron or a special grade of steel, but for light work it is sometimes of cast iron. The horn (*B*) must be tough in order to withstand heavy pounding and is usually of the same material as the body. The base of the horn (*C*) has a flat top which is used in preference to the face when cutting stock with a chisel, because it is not so hard and will not dull the chisel. The face (D) is a tool-steel plate $\frac{1}{2}$-inch thick which is welded to the body. It is carefully hardened and has a smoothly ground top. The square hardie hole (E) is used for holding the shanks of tools, while the pritchel hole (F) is very convenient in making small bolts, as it allows their stems, or shanks, to extend thru. The two side edges of the face (G) are rounded for about 4 inches near the horn, to facilitate the bending of stock. If intended for small work, like the exercises in this book, an anvil should weigh about 150 pounds.

The anvil should be placed with the horn at the left of the worker and the face 26 inches above the floor, the outer edge being about $\frac{1}{4}$ inch lower than the inner one. It is therefore necessary to provide a base. This is generally of cast iron, as shown in Fig. 2, but may consist of a large wooden block.

Fig. 3. TOOL-RACK.

Tool-Rack.—To have the blacksmith tools within easy reach while working at the forge, they should be kept on some sort of a tool-rack. A very good type is shown in Fig. 3. It consists of an iron top cast on one end of a piece of large pipe. The other end of the pipe is imbedded in the floor. Slots for holding tools are provided on each side of the top, which acts as a table for pieces of stock, supplies, etc.

These racks are sometimes made of wood, but such are easily burned by hot materials, and, since they usually have four legs and a bottom shelf, it is rather hard to clean under them.

The **Hammer** used most commonly by blacksmiths is a ball-peen hammer weighing from $1\frac{1}{2}$ to $2\frac{1}{2}$ pounds and similar to the one shown in Fig. 4. The face, or large end, is for ordinary work; and the ball end, or peen, for scarfing, riveting, etc. The face should be convex, in order not to mark hot material, and its edges rounded off, to keep them from breaking. The edge of the face nearest the worker is called the heel, and the front edge the toe.

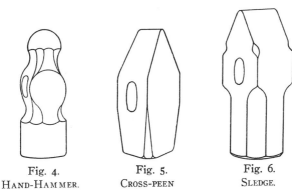

| Fig. 4. | Fig. 5. | Fig. 6. |
| HAND-HAMMER. | CROSS-PEEN | SLEDGE. |

A **Backing Hammer** generally has the same shape as the common ball-peen hammer, but it weighs about 5 pounds. It is used by a helper when light quick blows are necessary, and also when backing up, or starting, the heel of a scarf.

A **Cross-peen Hammer,** Fig. 5, weighing about $3\frac{1}{2}$ pounds, is needed for each two forges. This hammer is particularly valuable in welding steel on account of the heavier blows which can be delivered. It is also useful when making a pair of tongs, and in almost any work where one student needs the help of another.

Sledges.—Fig. 6 shows a sledge of the straight-peen type, which is ordinarily used in a blacksmith shop. The weight of such sledges varies from 8 to 13 pounds.

Tongs vary in form, depending on the size and shape of the stock handled. Those frequently used in the forge shop are shown in Fig. 7.

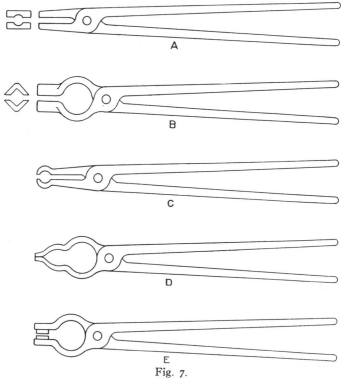

Fig. 7.

A, flat-jawed; *B,* hollow-bits; *C,* link; *D,* pick-ups; *E,* chisel.

The **Flat-Jawed Tongs,** shown at *A* in Fig. 7, are used for holding flat stock.

The **Hollow-Bit Tongs** (*B,* Fig. 7) are employed in handling round, square, or flat material.

Link Tongs are shown at *C*, Fig. 7, and are very convenient for holding links or rings.

Pick-up Tongs (*D*, Fig. 7) are intended mainly for picking up large and small pieces of different sizes of stock.

The **Eye Tongs,** or eye-chisel tongs, shown at *E* in Fig. 7, are used in dressing an eye-chisel. The projections are made to fit into the eye, while the jaws are bent so as to avoid contact with the burred head of the chisel.

Fitting Tongs to the Work.—Tongs should always be fitted to the work which they are intended to hold. The poorly fitted tongs shown at *A*, Fig. 8, should be changed so that the jaws touch the stock for their entire length, as in *B*, Fig. 8. Their form at *A* affords a poor grip, which is a serious drawback when forging or welding.

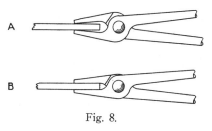

Fig. 8.

To fit tongs to a piece of work the jaws should be heated red hot, the stock placed between them, and the jaws hammered down tight around it. In order to prevent the handles, or reins, from coming too close together while doing this, a piece of iron should be placed between them directly behind the jaws. If the handles are too far apart, give them several blows a short distance back of the eye.

Never leave tongs on a piece of work while it is in the fire if there is danger of their becoming hot. When removed from the fire they will not hold the work firmly, because the handles will come together under the pressure of the hand.

Measuring and Marking Tools.—In forging it is often required to work to a given size, or to duplicate another forging. For this reason it is necessary to have on hand a rule, a pair of calipers, and a try-square, as shown in Fig. 9.

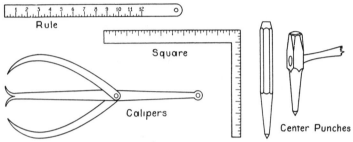

Fig. 9. MEASURING AND MARKING TOOLS.

The rule should be of brass in order to withstand the heat, and should have a 12-inch scale with enough extra room for a hand-hold. The calipers are generally made of steel, and are used mainly for work done under the trip-hammer. The try-square need only be a small one.

For marking stock a center-punch is generally employed,

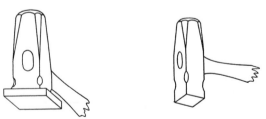

Fig. 10. THE FLATTER.   Fig. 11. THE SET-HAMMER.

since the mark made by a chisel will start a crack if the stock is bent. A chisel should be used only when the stock is to be cut off at the point marked.

The **Flatter**, Fig. 10, is used for flattening and smoothing straight surfaces. Its face is generally about 3 inches square, and should be smooth with rounded edges.

The **Set-Hammer**, shown in Fig. 11, is used in finishing corners and parts that cannot be reached with the flatter. The sizes vary, but for small work the face should be about 1¼ inches square. It also should be smooth and flat. The one illustrated is commonly called the square-edge set-hammer, to distinguish it from the round-edge set-hammer.

Chisels.—Two kinds of chisels are commonly used in the forge shop: one for cutting cold material, and the other for cutting hot material. These are called cold and hot chisels.

The cold chisel, Fig. 12, is made thicker in the blade than the hot chisel, Fig. 13, which has a rather thin edge. The

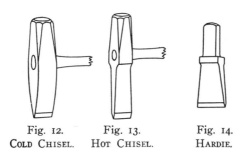

Fig. 12.   Fig. 13.   Fig. 14.
COLD CHISEL.   HOT CHISEL.   HARDIE.

hardie, shown in Fig. 14, is used for cutting hot material. It has a square shank to fit the hardie hole in the anvil. Hardies are also made to cut cold stock.

The hot chisel should never be used on cold material, as its edge will be turned and ruined; nor should the cold chisel be used for cutting hot stock, as the heat will soften its edge, making it unfit for cutting cold stock.

Grinding Chisels.—The sides of a cold chisel should be ground to an angle of about 60 degrees with each other, as shown at *A* in Fig. 15. This forms a good cutting edge. If the edge is too thin it will bend.

The cutting edge should also be ground convex, as shown slightly exaggerated at *B*. This prevents the corners from breaking off too readily, as they would if it were ground as at *C*.

Hot chisels are ground somewhat thinner than cold chisels, and with the sides at an angle of about 30°.

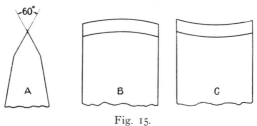

Fig. 15.

The **Bob-Punch,** shown in Fig. 16, is used in place of the peen of a hammer for hollowing out stock. Examples of its application are given in several of the special welds described in Chapter IV. It is hit with a heavy hammer, in the same manner as the flatter. If a hand hammer were used in place of the bob-punch its hardened face might break when struck.

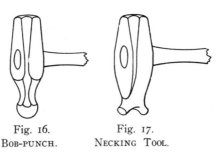

Fig. 16.   Fig. 17.
Bob-punch.   Necking Tool.

Necking Tool.—In certain cases, such as welding an eye-bolt, finishing the inside of the eye of a forged hook, and making a T-weld, a necking tool (Fig. 17) is very convenient, but not absolutely necessary.

Fullers.—Fig. 18 shows top and bottom fullers, which are used in forming grooves and filleted corners. They are made in a number of sizes, depending upon the radius of the circular edge, C. On a ¾-inch fuller this radius would be ⅜ inch.

The top fuller, A, is made with a handle, while the bottom fuller, B, has a square shank, like the hardie.

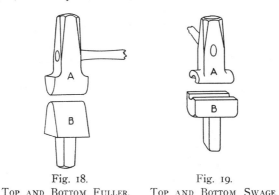

Fig. 18.
TOP AND BOTTOM FULLER.

Fig. 19.
TOP AND BOTTOM SWAGE.

Swages.—A top and a bottom swage are shown at A and B in Fig. 19. They are used for a wide variety of purposes, but mainly for finishing round material. The sizes vary accord-

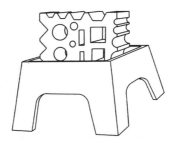

Fig. 20. THE SWAGE BLOCK.

ing to the diameter of the round stock for which they are made. Thus a 2-inch swage is used on 2-inch round stock.

A Swage Block is shown in Fig. 20. These blocks are usually made of cast iron, and, owing to their wide range of utility, in various shapes and sizes. They are of special importance in small shops, as they can be made to take the place of numerous swages and special tools. A cast-iron base is generally provided, as shown, on which they can be placed in either a flat or an upright position.

Vise.—For work requiring twisting and filing, some kind of a vise is desirable. The type most commonly used in a forge shop is shown in Fig. 21. A vise should always be attached to a firm and substantial bench.

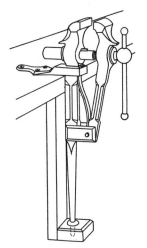

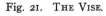

Fig. 21. THE VISE.   Fig. 22. THE CONE.

The **Cone**, Fig. 22, is used for rounding, or truing, rings. This is done by heating the rings thruout and forcing them down on the cone. If the ring is made in the form of a band from flat stock, it must be turned over and both edges expanded equally to make it straight.

Cones are made of cast iron in various sizes. A convenient one is from 2½ to 3½ feet high, with the diameter of the small end 2 inches and of the large end about 14 inches.

The **Surface Plate** suitable for technical schools is made of cast iron, and is about 2 by 3 feet, varying in thickness from 2 to 4 inches. It should have a number of 1¼-inch round or square holes in it, spaced about 3 inches between centers.

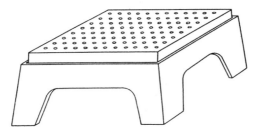

Fig. 23. THE SURFACE PLATE.

These are used for holding pins and formers when bending rings, pipes, and work similar in character. The face of the plate should be planed, so that work can be straightened or tested on it.

These plates are usually mounted on cast iron bases, as shown in Fig. 23; but wooden blocks may be used.

Shears.—For cutting off cold stock, shears are generally used in preference to a hardie or chisel, on account of the time which may be saved. They are either hand- or power-operated, and vary in size, being usually designated by the maximum size of stock which can be cut. One that should meet most of the demands of a technical school will cut ¾ x 4 inch stock. When material is cut with the shears, its ends are rough and have to be squared up on the anvil.

CHAPTER II.

Drawing-out, Bending, and Twisting.

Oxidizing Fire.—As the coal in a forge burns it consumes oxygen from the air-blast. If too much air is blown thru the fire there will be an excess of oxygen. This will attack the heated iron or steel, forming scale, or oxide of iron. The rate of this scale formation increases with the rise in temperature of the material.

Scale should be avoided even on an ordinary forging, since it pits the material and, if not removed while hot, makes it look as though it had been overheated. Unless the scale is in a molten condition it is also impossible to make a sound weld.

To Prevent the Formation of Scale the following precautions should be taken:

1. Have a good bed of hot coals over the tuyere iron for the air to pass thru.

2. Keep the material well covered with coke, in order to make the part of its surface exposed to the air as small as possible. If the air-blast comes in direct contact with the material, scale will form and the material will be cooled to a certain extent.

3. Do not put on too much blast, *i. e.,* force too much air thru the fire. If this is done the hot coals will be blown out of the center of the fire, leaving no bed of hot coals for consuming the oxygen.

Welding Heat.—When pieces of wrought iron are heated they soften, until at a certain temperature they will stick together if placed in contact. The temperature at which this soft and sticky condition occurs is known as the welding heat of wrought iron.

Soft steel has the required welding characteristics at a

lower temperature than wrought iron. It does not, however, become very soft at this heat.

Indications of a Welding Heat.—Just before the iron reaches the welding heat, explosive sparks will fly out of the fire. These sparks are small particles of the material which have melted off and are being blown out.

To reach this condition and have the material of uniform temperature thruout, the heating must be done slowly. If too much air-blast is used the outside of the material will burn as just described but the center will remain hard. An attempt to weld two pieces heated in this manner will generally result in a failure, since the cold inside together with the surrounding air will quickly cool the outside surface.

Burned Iron.—If a bar of wrought iron, or mild steel, be allowed to remain in the fire with the blast on after the welding heat has been reached, it will burn. The material which is burned off runs over the tuyere and forms lumps similar to the clinker. Since the burned portion of an iron bar is absolutely useless, care should be taken to remove the bar when it has reached the welding heat.

The air-blast should always be turned off when the material is removed from the fire. This prevents a waste of coal and keeps the fire small.

Drawing-Out is the process of increasing the length of a piece of stock while reducing its cross-sectional area. With machine steel this can be done at a yellow heat, but wrought iron requires a welding heat.

When the stock is at the proper heat, this drawing-out can be accomplished by hammering it over the large part of the horn with a hand hammer, as shown in Fig. 24. This makes the piece increase in length without widening it very much. If it were hammered on the face of the anvil a large amount of energy would be wasted, due to the sidewise spreading of the stock.

In drawing-out stock of any shape it should first be hammered square to prevent it from bursting. This also makes the grain finer and improves the physical properties of the material. Even when a round bar is to be reduced in diameter

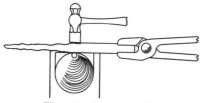

Fig. 24. DRAWING-OUT.

it should be first hammered square, then octagonal, and finally round.

The reason for this procedure can be explained with the aid of Fig. 25, which shows the cross-section of a piece of round stock that is being slowly revolved while hammering. The blows on top will cause the stock to flatten out and assume the shape indicated by the dotted line. This will make the sides, A and A, tend to pull away from the center. As

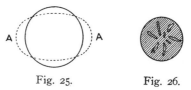

Fig. 25.   Fig. 26.

the piece is revolved and hammered the direction of this pull will change, so that the tendency will be for the whole outside surface to separate from the center. The result is the formation of cracks, as shown in Fig. 26. These make the iron structurally weak.

When drawing stock down to a conical point, as in Exercise 3, it must first be hammered square and the corners then rounded off. If this is not done the point will split or burst.

Squaring, or Truing-up, Work.—When drawing-out a

round bar to a square one there is danger of its becoming diamond-shaped in cross-section, as shown in Fig. 27. It will, in fact, almost invariably assume this shape if the bar is not heated uniformly. The bar may be trued-up by laying it across the anvil and striking it as indicated by the arrow so as to force the extra metal back into the body of the bar.

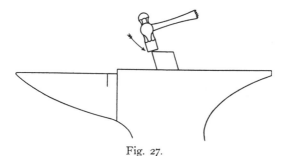

Fig. 27.

Cutting Cold Stock.—In cutting cold bars of soft steel or wrought iron with a cold chisel the method employed should be as follows: Around the bar make a series of cuts about one-fourth of the way thru, taking care to have them always at right angles to the axis of the bar. Tilt the bar slightly, and place the partly cut section at the outer edge of the anvil. By hitting the projecting end a sharp blow with a sledge it should break off easily.

If the stock becomes slightly warm when being cut in this way, cool it with water; otherwise it will be tough and will not break off.

Cutting Hot Stock.—Hot stock must be cut all the way thru, since it is generally too soft to be very easily broken off by a sledge blow. To obtain a square cut at one end of a bar the hot chisel should be tilted away from that end until one side of the cutting edge is perpendicular to the bar. Hot stock is usually cut from either two or four sides, but if it is flat the cutting is done from either one or both of the wider sides. In cutting round stock the bar should be revolved toward the worker.

The cutting edge of a hot chisel will become soft and bend if allowed to get too hot. For this reason it is necessary to dip it in water frequently to cool it off. It should also be removed from the cut between blows.

In using a chisel, and especially a hot chisel, never allow its cutting edge to come in contact with the hard face of the anvil. When a piece has been nearly cut thru, it should be moved forward until the cut is just outside the edge of the anvil. A copper plate is sometimes used for protecting the chisel edge when cutting thin stock. The chisel may then cut thru the stock and sink into the copper without having its edge spoiled.

A hardie is used in much the same manner as a chisel. When the stock has been nearly cut thru, the last blow or two should fall on the far side of the hardie. This keeps the face

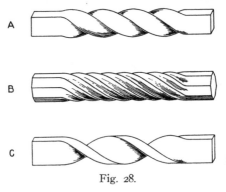

Fig. 28.

of the hammer from coming in contact with and spoiling the cutting edge of the hardie. It also prevents the projecting end from flying up and hitting the worker in the face, as it might if this were not done.

Twisting.—When twisting stock, it should first be marked with a center-punch at the points where the twist is to begin and end. The section to be twisted is heated to an even yellow heat. The piece is then quickly placed in a vise with one center-punch mark in line with one edge of the jaws, as shown in Fig. B, Plate V. A pair of flat-jawed tongs or a wrench is used to grasp the piece at the other mark in the same manner. The bar can then be twisted as much as required. If there is no vise convenient, two pairs of tongs may be used.

In order to obtain a uniform twist the stock must be uniformly heated. *A*, *B* and *C* of Fig. 28 illustrate the effects produced by twisting square, octagonal, and flat material respectively.

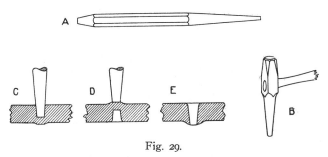

Fig. 29.

Punching.—Two kinds of punches are commonly employed for punching holes in hot material. The straight hand-punch shown at *A* in Fig. 29 is used on thin stock, while the eye-punch at *B* is used for punching holes in heavier stock. These punches should be made of tool steel, since they bend too easily if made of machine steel.

When punching thick material, the hot stock is laid flat on the anvil and the punch driven into it with a sledge-hammer. At a depth of about ¼ inch the punch is removed and some green or dry coal placed in the hole to prevent sticking. When the punch has been driven three-fourths of the way thru, as shown at *C*, a black mark will appear on the bottom side.

The stock is then reversed and the punching continued from that side, as at *D*. During the entire operation the punch should be cooled occasionally, to keep it from softening and bending. Care should be taken when finishing the punching to have the punch directly above the hardie or the pritchel hole, in order to allow the plug to drop thru.

A clean-cut hole will be obtained if this procedure is carried out; but if the punching is done from one side only, a burr will be raised on the lower side, as shown at *E*.

Exercise 1.   Drawing-out and Bending Ring.   (Plate I.)

This exercise is given for the purpose of familiarizing the student with the heating of machine steel or wrought iron and the use of the hand-hammer.

STEP ONE.—The round stock is drawn out square, as shown at 1. This is done by heating about 3 or 4 inches of it at one end to a yellow heat, and reducing it with a hand-hammer on the large part of the horn, as shown in Fig. 24.

STEP TWO.—The material is rounded by hammering it on the corners, making it first octagonal and then round. It is smoothed up either by placing it in a ½-inch bottom-swage and revolving it while hammering or by using top- and bottom-swages.

STEP THREE.—A piece 11⅜ inches long is cut off of the drawn-out portion. This may be done on the hardie in the manner already described. Be sure to have the last blows fall on the far side of the hardie, to avoid spoiling its edge and to prevent the cut portion from flying up into the face of the worker.

STEP FOUR.—About a third of the stock is heated, and bent over the large part of the anvil, as shown at 4. The hammer blows should fall on the end outside of the horn, and not on top of the horn. This will bend the material without marring it. The other end is bent in the same manner.

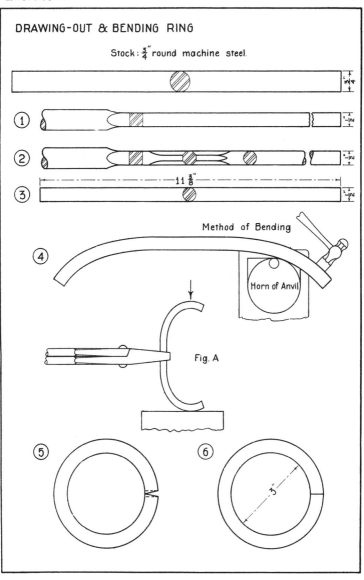

DRAWING-OUT & BENDING RING

Stock: $\frac{3}{4}$" round machine steel.

Method of Bending

Horn of Anvil

Fig. A

STEP FIVE.—The piece is heated and held with a pair of link-tongs, as shown in Fig. A. The bending is then continued by hammering as indicated. The ring is finally made circular on the horn of the anvil. The ends must be cut off with a hot chisel or hardie along the dotted lines shown.

STEP SIX.—The ends are driven together and the rounding finished. When the ring is completed, it may be given a black finish by holding it over a smoky fire until black hot and then wiping it with oily waste.

Exercise 2. S-Hook. (Plate II.)

STEP ONE.—After squaring up the ends of the stock, heat about half of the piece and bend one end over the horn. Be sure to have the blows fall on the far side of the horn, as in the previous exercise.

STEP TWO.—Continue the bending until the piece is shaped as shown.

STEP THREE.—Heat the other end and bend it over the horn in the same manner as before, but in the opposite direction.

STEP FOUR.—Complete the bending by making the hook appear as shown. The finished hook should be free from rough marks caused by improper bending.

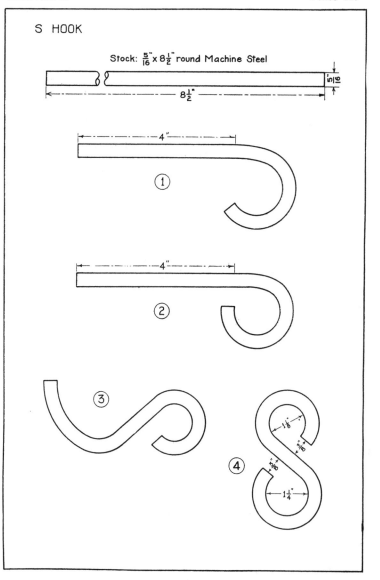

S HOOK

Stock: $\frac{5}{16}$" x 8$\frac{1}{2}$" round Machine Steel

8$\frac{1}{2}$"

$\frac{5}{16}$"

4"

①

4"

②

③

④

1$\frac{1}{8}$"

$\frac{5}{8}$"

$\frac{5}{8}$"

1$\frac{1}{4}$"

Exercise 3.   Staples.   (Plate III.)

STEP ONE.—Cut the stock to length, then hammer out the ends to a square or a chisel-point, as shown at 1*a* and 1*b*. Work at the outer edge of the anvil, to avoid hitting the anvil face with the hand-hammer.   Both anvil and hammer faces may be chipped or broken if this is not done.

STEP TWO.—Heat the stock at the center and bend it over the horn, taking care to have the blows fall on the outside.

STEP THREE.—Finish the bending operation, and cut off the ends with a hardie.   If the ends are crooked they may be straightened on the hardie, as shown in Fig. 30.

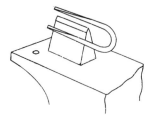

Fig. 30.

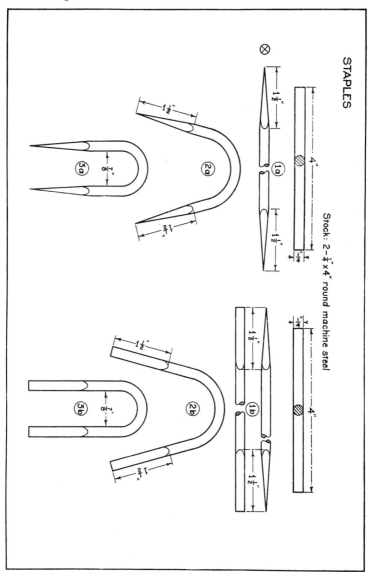

STAPLES

Stock: 2 – ¼" x 4" round machine steel

Exercise 4. Beam Strap. (Plate IV.)

STEP ONE.—As with any bent shape, the length of stock required for this exercise is determined by measuring along the center line of the finished shape, *i. e.*, along the dotted line in 3. The location of the right-angle bend and the beginning and end of the twist should be marked with a center-punch. This is done on the edge of the stock before it is heated. A cold chisel should not be used for marking, since the cut expands and starts a crack.

STEP TWO.—Take a short high heat at the center-punch mark where the piece is to be bent, and lay the stock on the anvil at the rounded edge, as shown in Fig. A. The center-punch mark should not come quite in line with the outer edge of the anvil, for the stock has a tendency to move forward during the bending operation. In order to make the bend as short as possible the bar should be firmly held down on the anvil with a sledge. Strike the end as indicated, and bend the stock to a right angle.

STEP THREE.—Square up the corner by placing the exercise on the anvil, as in Fig. B, and striking it in the manner indicated by the arrows. It should also be reversed on the anvil and struck on the end, as shown in Fig. C. By striking at E the stock is made thicker at F, forming a fillet on the inside corner. Care should be taken during this operation to keep the angle at or greater than 90° lest the stock be upset, as in Fig. D, forming a cold-shut or crack on the inside corner. This would make the angle weak. After the corner has been upset and hammered to shape, it is smoothed up with a flatter.

Caution.—Do not try to square the stock by placing it over a corner of the anvil, as it will then be hammered too thin.

STEP FOUR.—Take a uniform yellow heat on the stock, and place one end in a vise. Give it a quarter-turn with a pair of flat-jawed tongs in the manner already described.

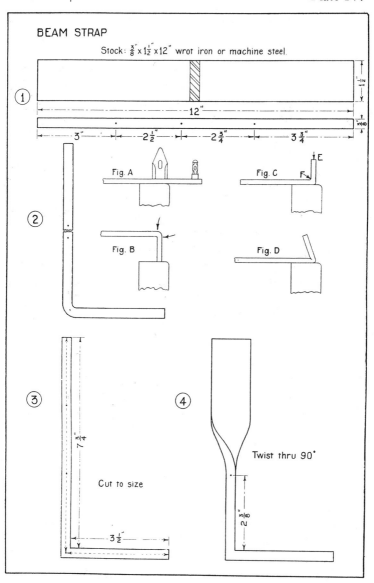

BEAM STRAP

Stock: $\frac{3}{8}'' \times 1\frac{1}{2}'' \times 12''$ wrot iron or machine steel.

① 12"

$1\frac{1}{2}''$

$\frac{3}{8}''$

3" 2½" 2¾" 3¾"

② Fig. A Fig. C E F

Fig. B Fig. D

③ 7¾"

Cut to size

3½"

④ Twist thru 90°

2⅜"

Exercise 5. Twisted Gate-Hook. (Plate V.)

STEP ONE.—Cut a piece of $\frac{5}{16}$-inch square machine steel to the size indicated, and mark it with a center-punch, as shown at 1.

STEP TWO.—To form a shoulder, heat one end of the stock and place it with the center-punch mark directly above the inner edge of the anvil. Rest the set-hammer on top of the piece so that its side edge is in line with the edge of the anvil, as in Fig. A. The stock should then be turned while the set-hammer is being hit, or the shoulder will be worked in faster on one side than on another. Care should be taken to keep the shoulder exactly even with the edge of the anvil.

STEP THREE.—When the shoulder has been formed, as shown at the end D in 2, the end is hammered out square and then round. It is finished between top- and bottom-swages. The other end of the piece is shouldered and drawn out in the same manner. If the shoulder is not square, it may be trued up by inserting the swaged end in a heading-tool, as shown in Fig. B, and striking on the opposite end of the stock.

The end D is then pointed by hammering it to a square point, rounding off the corners, and cutting it to length.

STEP FOUR.—To bend the eye, the stock is heated uniformly and the bend started over the rounded edge of the anvil. The square stock at the shoulder should be cooled, to prevent its bending. The eye is finished on the horn of the anvil in the same manner as the S-hook.

The hook is bent in much the same way. About $\frac{1}{2}$ inch of the point should be cooled and the blows allowed to fall on this cold part, in order to avoid marring the stock.

STEP FIVE.—Before twisting the middle section, center-punch marks should be made $1\frac{1}{2}$ inches from each shoulder, leaving $1\frac{1}{2}$ inches between these marks. This portion is heated to an even yellow and placed in a vise, as shown in Fig. C. With the aid of a pair of flat-jawed tongs the stock is given one complete turn.

The hook should be filed while hot, to remove the scale, and then blackened.

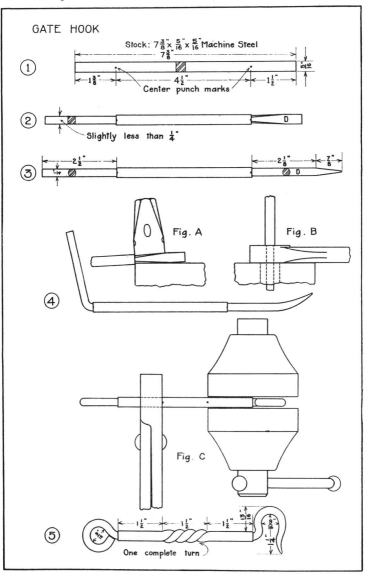

GATE HOOK

Stock: $7\frac{3}{8}'' \times \frac{5}{16}'' \times \frac{5}{16}''$ Machine Steel

① $7\frac{3}{8}''$ ... $\frac{5}{16}''$ ... $1\frac{3}{8}''$ ... $4\frac{1}{2}''$ ... $1\frac{1}{2}''$
Center punch marks

② Slightly less than $\frac{1}{4}''$ ... D

③ $2\frac{1}{2}''$ ... $\frac{1}{4}''$ ... $2\frac{1}{8}''$ ... $\frac{7}{8}''$ ... D

④ Fig. A   Fig. B

Fig. C

⑤ $1\frac{1}{2}''$ ... $1\frac{1}{2}''$ ... $1\frac{1}{2}''$ ... $\frac{13}{16}''$ ... $\frac{9}{16}''$ ... $\frac{1}{4}''$
One complete turn

CHAPTER III

COMMON WELDS.

The **Lap-Weld** is the one ordinarily used for joining flat, square, or round bars. In order that the cross-section of the material at the weld be the same as that of the stock, it is generally necessary to upset the ends before welding.

Upsetting.—When the length of a piece of stock is decreased and its cross-sectional area increased at any point, it is said to be upset at that point. Before this can be done to the end of a piece of wrought iron, it is necessary to bring it to a welding heat. A section in the middle of the stock does not have to be heated so much. If the upsetting is to be at one end, the stock should first be hammered on all sides, to prevent it from bursting thru the slag seams at the end. When the end of a short piece is to be upset, it may be done by holding the piece vertically with a pair of link-tongs, the hot end resting on the face of the anvil, and striking the top end with a hand-hammer. Heavy blows are necessary, and as they have a tendency to bend the stock it must be straightened occasionally. The end of a long piece may be upset by gripping the cold end with the hands and striking the hot one against the face of the anvil.

The object of upsetting a piece before welding is to make allowance for the iron which is lost thru scaling and burning, and for the drawing-out caused by the hammering required for a sound weld. If the stock is hammered out too thin at the weld, it may be upset again at that point, but this is a more difficult operation than upsetting before welding. It is therefore better to upset the ends of the original bar too much than not enough, as the surplus stock can very quickly be hammered out. The amount of upsetting required depends entirely upon the number of heats taken in welding. Every time a bar of iron is brought to the welding heat there is a portion of the outside surface wasted on account of scaling and burning. The amount of material allowed for waste in welding therefore depends upon the number of heats required to make a sound weld. This allowance is generally from one-fourth to three-fourths of the diameter of the stock.

Scarfing is the process of shaping the ends of stock so that when they are welded together a smooth joint will be obtained. The shapes of these scarfs depend to a large extent upon the character of the weld, and will be taken up in detail in Exercises 6 to 16. In general the parts of the scarfs which are placed in contact in welding should be convex, as shown at 3 in Plate VII. The two centers will then touch first, and the molten oxide will be allowed to escape. If the scarfs were made concave this oxide could not escape or be squeezed out, and the weld would be a poor and unsound one.

Use of Fluxes in Welding.—When heating a piece of common iron or steel for welding, oxidation takes place and a thin film of oxide of iron is formed on the surface. This oxide, or scale, must be heated to a high temperature before becoming fluid enough to run off and permit a sound weld.

Wrought iron may be heated enough to melt off this oxide without being burned, but steel would be injured if brought to such a high temperature. It is therefore necessary, when welding both high- and low-carbon steel, to use a flux, such as powdered borax, in order to lower the melting point of the oxide. A flux is also often used when welding wrought iron, but is not essential. Fluxes do not act as cements, but merely make the iron weldable at a lower temperature.

Method of Using Flux.—After the pieces in the fire have reached a yellow heat, some flux is thrown or sprinkled on the scarfs, or parts to be welded, and the heating continued up to the welding heat. As the flux melts it flows over the scarf, forming a coat or covering. This dissolves the oxide already formed and prevents further oxidation.

The flux used when welding wrought iron is generally clean, sharp sand. There are various welding compounds on the market, some of which contain borax and iron filings. Most of them contain borax, and are used mainly when welding steel.

Exercise 6.   Practice Welds—Fagot.   (Plate VI.)

The **Fagot Weld** is given as an exercise in order that the student may (1) become familiar with welding heats, (2) learn to use the hand-hammer effectively, (3) have further practice in the drawing-out of wrought iron, (4) and also for economy, since old links, rings, or pieces of scrap iron may be used to good advantage.

This weld may be made by placing two or more pieces of iron on top of each other and welding them for their entire length. Another method is to bend the end of a piece of stock once or twice, as in 1a and 2a, and weld it into a solid lump.

If a link or ring is available, it can be heated and closed for half its length, as in 3a. This portion is then welded and hammered out square. When the other end has been treated in the same manner, the entire piece is hammered octagonal, then round, and finally smoothed up between top- and bottom-swages. This finished piece may be used again for making a ring or link.

Exercise 7.   Round Lap-Weld.   (Plate VII.)

STEP ONE.—Upset one end of each of two pieces of round stock for about 2 inches, as shown at 1. This is done by heating the ends to a welding heat and hitting them against the face of the anvil, in the manner already described.

STEP TWO.—The scarf is started by placing the stock on the face of the anvil, with the upset portion near the rounded

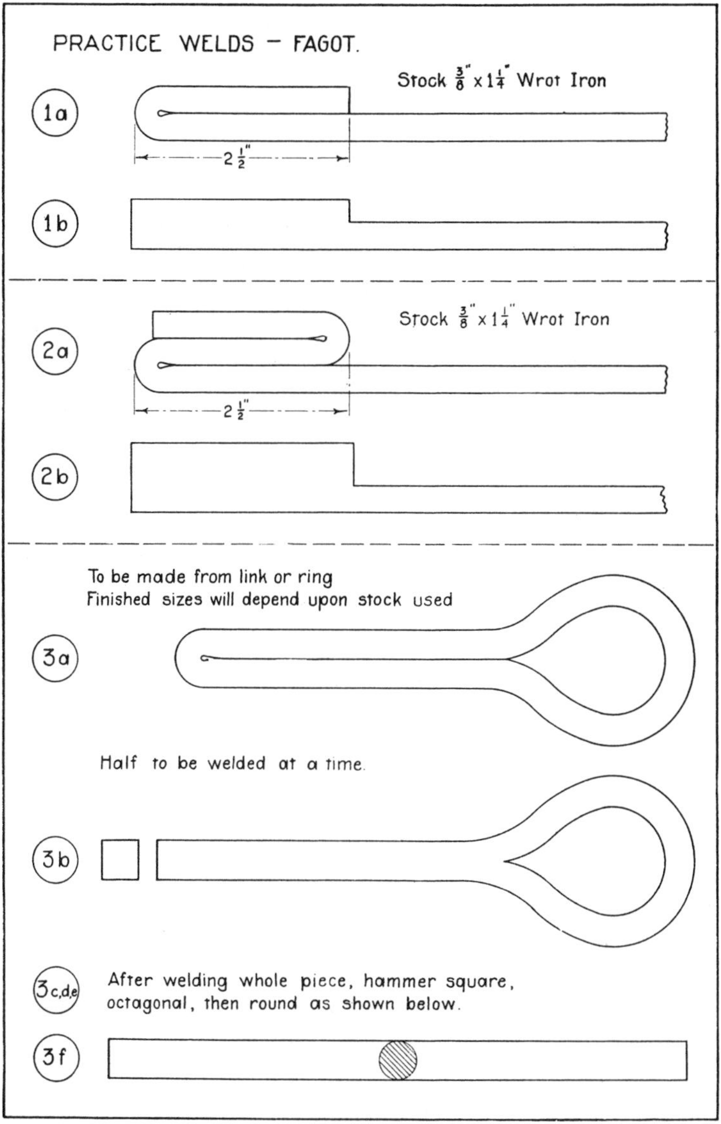

PRACTICE WELDS — FAGOT.

Stock $\frac{3}{8}$" x $1\frac{1}{4}$" Wrot Iron

(1a)

$2\frac{1}{2}$"

(1b)

Stock $\frac{3}{8}$" x $1\frac{1}{4}$" Wrot Iron

(2a)

$2\frac{1}{2}$"

(2b)

To be made from link or ring
Finished sizes will depend upon stock used

(3a)

Half to be welded at a time.

(3b)

(3c,d,e) After welding whole piece, hammer square,
octagonal, then round as shown below.

(3f)

edge, and hitting it with the face of a hand-hammer. After a few blows the peen is used, as shown in Fig. A. These blows should come at an angle of about 45°, in order to force the material back and form a thick ridge at the heel of the scarf, as shown at 2. The scarf at this point should be slightly tapered.

STEP THREE.—The scarf is finished at the rounded edge of the anvil with the face of the hammer. This is done to avoid hitting the hammer against the sharp edge of the anvil. The length of the scarf should be about one and one-half times the thickness of the bar at the upset portion.

The scarf is worked down to a point, as shown at 3, in order to facilitate welding the end of the scarf. If these ends were very wide several blows would be necessary to weld them, and, since they cool very rapidly, considerable skill and speed would be required.

STEP FOUR.—When heating the stock for welding have a good bed of hot coals. Place the short piece at the right of the long one, the scarfs of both being face down, and cover them with coke. Heat slowly, to insure a uniform temperature thruout the scarfed portions. If one piece should heat faster than the other, pull it back a little from the center of the fire. Both pieces must be at a welding heat at the same time.

When at the welding heat remove the pieces from the fire, taking the short piece in the right hand and the long one in the left. Keeping the scarf side down, give them each a quick blow on the horn of the anvil, to dislodge any dirt on the faces of the scarfs. Place the short piece on the anvil with the scarf up, as shown in Fig. C. This piece is not so liable to overbalance and fall to the floor, as sometimes happens when welding without assistance, if the end of the scarf comes nearly to the inner edge of the anvil. Steady the scarfed end of the other piece against the edge of the anvil, as shown in

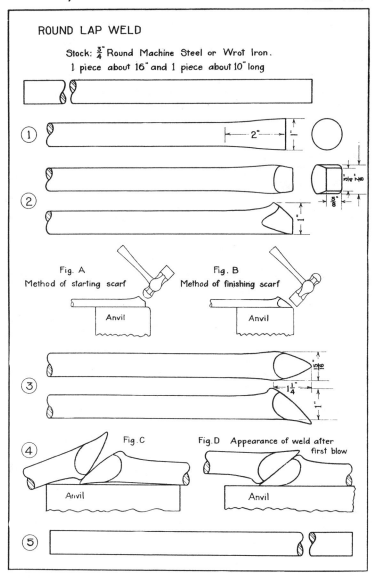

ROUND LAP WELD

Stock: ¾" Round Machine Steel or Wrot Iron.
1 piece about 16" and 1 piece about 10" long

(1) — 2" —

(2)

Fig. A
Method of starting scarf

Fig. B
Method of finishing scarf

Anvil

Anvil

(3) $\frac{15}{16}$" $1\frac{1}{4}$" 1"

(4) Fig. C

Fig. D Appearance of weld after first blow

Anvil

Anvil

(5)

Fig. C, and bring it to the desired position above the short piece. The end of one scarf should lap over the thick ridge, or heel, of the other, as in Fig. D.

With a hand-hammer deliver a few sharp blows, to stick the body of the material. The ends of the scarfs should then be hammered down, otherwise they will become too cold and will not stick. If the scarfs are not thoroughly welded at the first heat, put the piece back into the fire and take another welding heat on it.

STEP FIVE.—After the weld has been made, the scale should be cleaned off with a file, since it pits the material. The bar is then finished between top- and bottom-swages.

Exercise 8. Flat Lap-Weld. (Plate VIII.)

STEP ONE.—The stock is upset for about 2 inches in the manner previously described.

STEP TWO.—The scarf is started in the same way as for the round lap-weld. It should not, however, taper very much at the end.

STEP THREE.—The finished scarf should be made the same width as the bar at the thick ridge, and slightly tapered toward the end, as at 3.

STEP FOUR.—The two pieces are welded together in much the same manner as the round stock of Exercise 7. It is advisable, though, to use a heavy hand-hammer in welding flat bars.

STEP FIVE.—When the welding is finished, the scale should be cleaned off with a file and the piece smoothed up with a flatter.

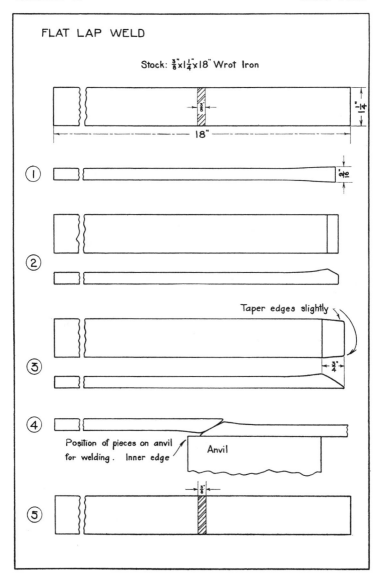

FLAT LAP WELD

Stock: ⅜"x1¼"x18" Wrot Iron

Taper edges slightly

Position of pieces on anvil for welding. Inner edge

Anvil

Exercise 9. Links of Chain. (Plate IX.)

The length of the material required for a link is found by measuring the distance around at the center of the stock. To compute this distance the desired link, shown at 4, should be separated into two semi-circular ends and two straight connecting sections. The mean diameter of the ends is $1\frac{1}{4}$ inches; so $1\frac{1}{4} \times 3\frac{1}{7}$, or $3\frac{15}{16}$ inches, is required for them. The connecting sections are each $1\frac{3}{8}$ inches long. The total length is then $3\frac{15}{16} + 2 \times 1\frac{3}{8} = 6\frac{11}{16}$ inches. To this should be added a small amount, about $\frac{1}{8}$ inch, for the waste in welding.

STEP ONE.—Square up the ends of the material, and heat the middle uniformly for about 3 inches. Bend it halfway on the horn, taking care to have the blows fall on the cold projecting end. It should then be reversed and the other end bent over in the same manner, forming a U, as shown at 1. The reason for this reversal is that if the U were formed by hitting on one end only that side of the U would be the shorter of the two. If one side should be longer than the other, it may be shortened by heating the semi-circular portion, placing it on a bottom-swage, the shorter leg being held vertical with a pair of link-tongs, and striking on the end of the longer leg.

STEP TWO.—The ends are brought to a yellow heat and scarfed by placing one end on the anvil, as shown at *A*, and striking a number of blows, moving the U toward the horn after each one. This leaves a series of notches on the under side of the piece, as shown at 2. The U is then turned over, and the other end treated in the same manner. The scarfs are finished on the face of the anvil with the peen or the heel of a hand-hammer. They should not be less than $\frac{1}{16}$ inch thick at the end, or they will cool too quickly and it will be almost impossible to weld them.

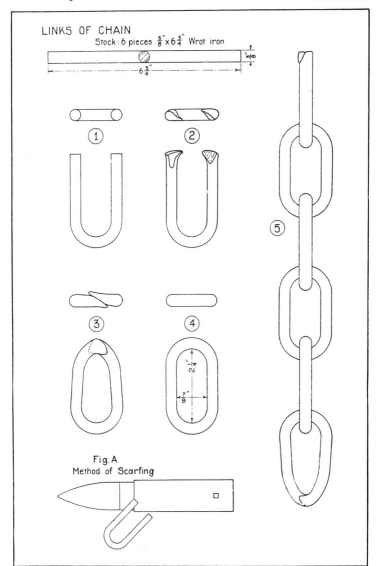

LINKS OF CHAIN
Stock: 6 pieces $\frac{3}{8}"$ × $6\frac{3}{4}"$ Wrot iron

$6\frac{3}{4}"$

$\frac{3}{8}"$

① ② ③ ④ ⑤

$2\frac{1}{4}"$

$\frac{7}{8}"$

Fig. A
Method of Scarfing

STEP THREE.—Bring the ends together, as at 3, taking care to have the end of the top scarf pointed toward the right. If it points to the left, the scarf is left-hand and is harder to weld. The link should be shaped so that the end to be welded is narrower than the other. The stock is then less liable to be hammered small on either side of the weld, and the semi-circular end will be about the right size when the weld is finished.

STEP FOUR.—Take a welding heat and weld the joint with a few quick blows of the hand-hammer. The link is finished on the horn of the anvil.

STEP FIVE.—When joining links, the connecting one is scarfed and its ends brought together ready for welding. The

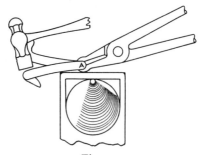

Fig. 31.

end *A* of the link is then heated, the scarfs spread apart, as shown in Fig. 31, the links slipped on, and the scarfs brought together again. This connecting link is welded in the same manner as the others.

Welded Ring.—A ring formed from round stock may be made in two ways, *i. e.,* by scarfing before or after bending it into shape. The second of these is the less difficult, as the scarfs are then more easily fitted and the stock on either side of the weld is not so likely to become thin.

The amount of material required to make it is computed

from its mean diameter. For the following two exercises this mean diameter is $3\frac{1}{4}$ inches, as shown in Plate X. The mean circumference of the ring is then $3\frac{1}{4} \times 3\frac{1}{7}$, or approximately $10\frac{1}{4}$ inches. To this must be added an allowance for waste in welding, depending on the number of heats necessary. For a student this would be about $\frac{3}{8}$ or $\frac{1}{2}$ inch, so the total length of stock required is $10\frac{3}{4}$ inches.

Exercise 10. Ring—Round Lap-Weld. (Plate X.)

STEP ONE.—Upset the ends of the stock until its length is 9⅜ inches.

STEP TWO.—Scarf the ends as shown at 2 in the same manner as for a simple lap-weld for round stock.

STEP THREE.—Heat one-third of the stock and bend it over the large part of the horn, keeping the straight side of the scarfed end toward the right. Strike on the projecting end, as shown, in order not to mar the material. The other end is bent in the same manner, making the exercise appear as shown at 3.

STEP FOUR.—Heat the center section and complete the bending by holding the piece upright on the anvil with a pair of link-tongs and knocking the scarfs together. The point of the top scarf should look toward the right, as at 4. If the scarfs do not meet squarely, shape the ring on the horn. Hammer the scarfs close together on the face of the anvil, so that no dirt can get in between them.

STEP FIVE.—Heat and weld the ring in the same manner as a link. When the welding is finished, smooth the ring on the horn of the anvil with a top-swage. To make the ring circular, heat it all over and drive it down on the cone with a hand-hammer.

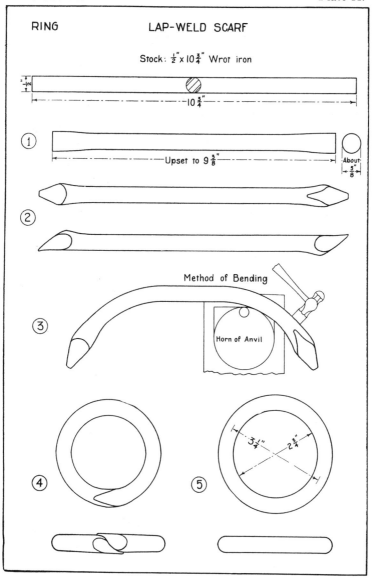

RING   LAP-WELD SCARF

Stock: $\frac{1}{2}"$ x 10$\frac{3}{4}"$ Wrot iron

$\frac{1}{2}"$

10$\frac{3}{4}"$

① Upset to 9$\frac{3}{8}"$ About $\frac{5}{8}"$

②

Method of Bending

③   Horn of Anvil

④   ⑤   3$\frac{1}{4}"$ 2$\frac{3}{4}"$

Exercise 11.   Ring—Link Scarf.   (Plate XI.)

STEP ONE.—Upset the ends of the stock until its length is 9⅝ inches.

STEP TWO.—Bend the ends to the form shown at 2 in the same manner as in the previous exercise.

STEP THREE.—Heat the middle section and bend the ends to within a short distance of each other, as at 3.

STEP FOUR.—Scarf the ends in the same way as for a link.

STEP FIVE.—Bring the scarfed ends together, as at 5.

STEP SIX.—Weld the two ends and finish the ring in the same manner as in the previous exercise.

Exercise 12.   Forged Hook.   (Plate XII.)

Forged hooks are made from tool steel, Norway iron, or machine steel.   The one in this exercise is to be made from ¾-inch round machine steel.

STEP ONE.—Cut the stock 6 inches long.   Heat about 1½ inches at one end to a yellow heat and upset it as at 1, decreasing its length to 5½ inches.   A longer piece may be used more advantageously, since the end can then be upset and the eye finished without the use of tongs.   If a long piece is used, care should be taken to mark it 6 inches from the end with a center-punch before upsetting.

STEP TWO.—Flatten the upset end until it is ½ inch thick, as at 2.

STEP THREE.—Use ½-inch top- and bottom-fullers or a necking-tool to fuller the neck to the form shown at 3.

STEP FOUR.—Round the end or head by placing one corner of it on the face of the anvil and using the necking-tool on the shoulder, as in Fig. 32.   Treat the other corner in the same manner.   Rounding may be finished with the hand-hammer by holding the piece over the rounded edge of the

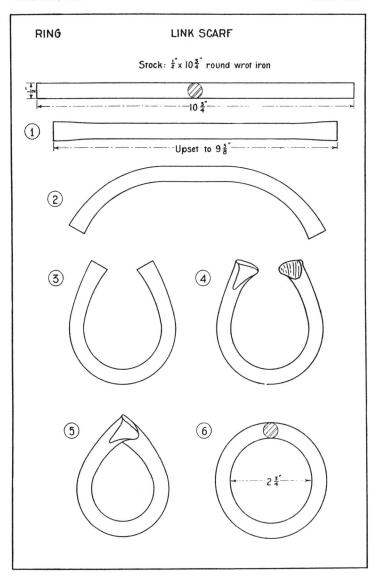

RING   LINK SCARF

Stock: $\frac{1}{2}$" x 10$\frac{3}{4}$" round wrot iron

10$\frac{3}{4}$"

① Upset to 9$\frac{5}{8}$"

②

③   ④

⑤   ⑥   2$\frac{3}{4}$"

anvil and striking it as shown in Fig. 33. This end should be forged as nearly round as practicable before the hole is punched in it.

STEP FIVE.—Punch a ⅜-inch hole in the forged end or head, as at 5, and draw the neck out square with the hand-hammer. While doing this allow the eye to extend over the rounded edge of the anvil, in order to prevent the filleted corners from becoming sharp.

STEP SIX.—Round the inside edges of the hole over the horn, as shown in Fig. 34, and finish or smooth the outside

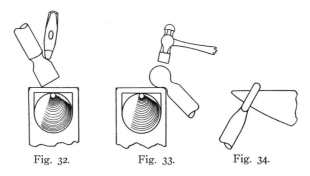

Fig. 32.　　　　Fig. 33.　　　　Fig. 34.

with a ½-inch top-swage. Make the hole circular by driving a tapered pin through it. The finished eye should then appear as though made from round stock.

The neck is hammered round and finished with ¾-inch tapered top- and bottom-swages. If, when this is done, the stock is too long, it should be cut to the length given at 6.

STEP SEVEN.—Draw down the end to a square point, working at the rounded edge of the anvil and holding the stock at such an angle with the anvil face as will bring the point in the center line.

STEP EIGHT.—Round off the corners of the point, as at 8. The length of a hook from the neck, or shoulder, of the eye to the extreme end should be eight times the diameter of its

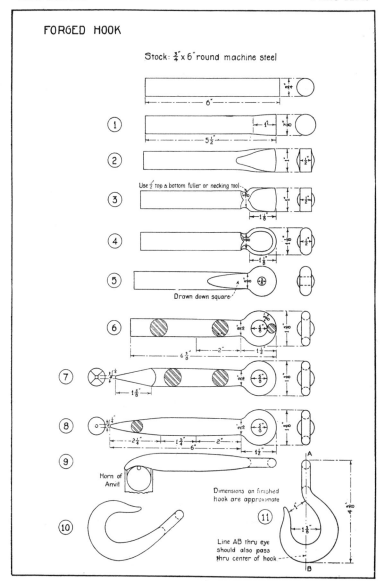

FORGED HOOK

Stock: $\frac{3}{4}$" x 6" round machine steel

①

②

③ Use $\frac{1}{2}$" top & bottom fuller or necking tool

④

⑤ Drawn down square

⑥

⑦

⑧

⑨ Horn of Anvil

⑩

⑪ Dimensions on finished hook are approximate

Line AB thru eye should also pass thru center of hook

largest cross-section. This length is 6 inches for the hook given.

STEP NINE.—Bend the point over the horn, as shown at 9.

STEP TEN.—In bending the hook, heat it for about 4 inches at the center, and cool the neck and point. Place it on the large part of the horn, with the cold tip projecting over. A sledge should be held on top of it, in order to prevent it from slipping over the horn too far when hit. Strike the projecting tip with a hand-hammer, moving the hook toward the point of the horn as the bending progresses. It should be bent to the form shown at 10. If it is necessary to change the shape of the hook on the horn, a top-swage should be used. This leaves the hook free from marks of the hand-hammer.

STEP ELEVEN.—Take a short heat at the neck and bend the eye back over the horn. The finished hook, shown at 11, should be heated and the scale removed with a file. It may then be attached with a link to the chain of Exercise 9.

Exercise 13. Common Eye-Bolt. (Plate XIII.)

STEP ONE.—Cut a piece of ½-inch round wrought iron 12¼ inches long. Heat one end to a welding heat and scarf it, as shown at 1.

STEP TWO.—Bend the scarf over the rounded edge of the anvil and mark it with a center-punch, as shown at 2.

STEP THREE.—Heat about 7 inches of the stock at the scarfed end to a uniform yellow heat. The bend is then started by placing the stock with the center-punch mark above the rounded edge of the anvil, and striking on the projecting end with the peen of a hand-hammer.

STEP FOUR.—Finish the bending on the horn, striking on the scarf, to avoid marring the stock.

STEP FIVE.—Place a drift-pin, or a piece of round stock

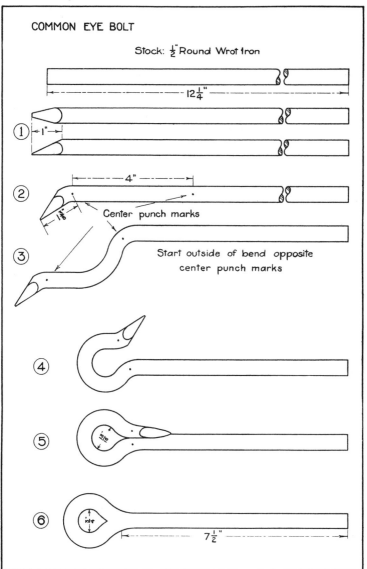

COMMON EYE BOLT

Stock: ½" Round Wrot Iron

① |← 1" →|

② ← 4" → Center punch marks

③ Start outside of bend opposite center punch marks

④

⑤

⑥ 7½"

slightly larger than the finished hole, in the eye and bring the scarf and shank together, as at 5.

STEP SIX.—Heat the stock slowly to a welding heat, and weld down the scarfed end. A necking-tool or a top-fuller is used in rounding the shoulder. The welding should be finished with a hand-hammer at the rounded edge of the anvil. Smooth up the stock at the weld with a top- and a bottom-swage, and drive a drift-pin into the hole to make it symmetrical. While still hot the scale should be removed with a file.

Fig. 35.

One of the commonest applications of this exercise is the clevis shown in Fig. 35. This is formed by making an eye at each end of a piece of stock, and bending it into the form of a U.

Exercise 14. Common Hinge. (Plate XIV.)

STEP ONE.—Scarf the end of a piece of wrought iron $\frac{1}{4} \times 1\frac{1}{4}$ inch $\times$ 11 inches, as shown at 1, and make a center-punch mark on one edge $4\frac{1}{2}$ inches from the end.

STEP TWO.—Heat about 5 inches of the piece at the scarfed end, and place it on the anvil with the scarfed side down. The center-punch mark should come almost in line with the outer rounded edge of the anvil. Bend as at 2.

STEP THREE.—Continue the bending on the horn, and close the eye on a pin which is slightly larger than the finished hole.

COMMON HINGE

Stock: $\frac{1}{4}$" x $1\frac{1}{4}$" x 11" Wrot iron

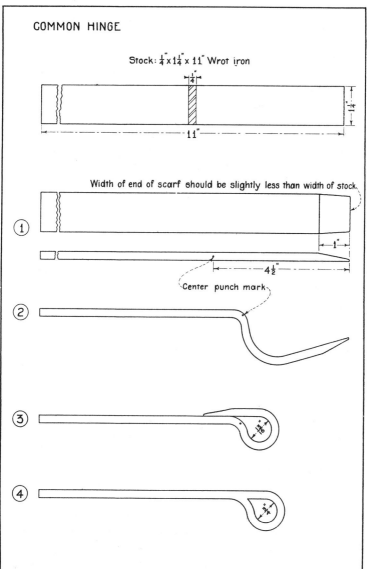

Width of end of scarf should be slightly less than width of stock

①

Center punch mark

②

③ $\frac{13}{16}$"

④ $\frac{3}{4}$"

STEP FOUR.—In placing the piece in the fire have the scarf down, in order to avoid burning the eye. When the piece is at the welding heat, it should be removed from the fire and laid on the anvil with the scarf up and the eye against the rounded edge of the anvil. If this were not done and it were welded over the sharp edge of the anvil, the neck would have a sharp corner instead of being rounded, as shown at 4. The welding is done with a heavy hand-hammer.

After the welding has been completed, a pin should be driven into the hole and a top-swage used to smooth the eye. A flatter may be used to smooth the stock at the weld.

Exercise 15. Flat Ring. (Plate XV.)

STEP ONE.—Cut a piece of $\frac{1}{4} \times 1\frac{1}{4}$-inch wrought iron 14 inches long, as shown, and heat one end for about $2\frac{1}{2}$ inches. Upset it at an angle, as shown at 1. If, while doing this, most of the upsetting occurs at the tip, the extreme end should be cooled off. To decrease the width at the upset portion it should be hammered on the longer edge at A. This will keep both edges the same in thickness. Upset the other end in the same manner.

STEP TWO.—Scarf the ends as shown at 2, taking care to have the scarfs on opposite sides of the stock.

STEP THREE.—Heat one end of the stock for about 4 inches, cool the corner B, and bend the end over the horn. The hammer blows should fall on B. Bend the other end in the same manner.

STEP FOUR.—Heat the center of the stock, and finish the bending in the same manner as for the ring in Exercise 1. The scarfs should come squarely together and be closed tightly, as at 4, to prevent dirt from getting in between them.

STEP FIVE.—Bring the scarfs slowly to the welding heat, and weld them together on the face of the anvil with a heavy

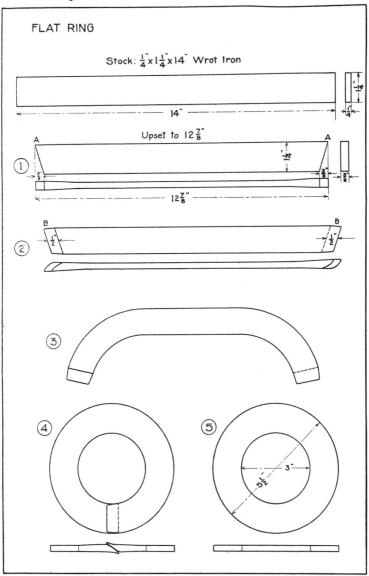

FLAT RING

Stock: $\frac{1}{4}" \times 1\frac{1}{4}" \times 14"$ Wrot Iron

14"

$1\frac{1}{4}"$

$\frac{1}{4}"$

Upset to $12\frac{7}{8}"$

① A   A

$1\frac{1}{4}"$

$12\frac{7}{8}"$

② B   B

$\frac{1}{2}"$ $\frac{1}{2}"$

③

④   ⑤

3"

$5\frac{1}{2}"$

hand-hammer. Finish the edges on the horn, then smooth the sides with a flatter. The ring should be made circular on a cone, and the scale removed with a file.

Exercise 16. Band Ring. (Plate XVI.)

STEP ONE.—Cut the stock to length, and upset each end for about 2 inches.

STEP TWO.—Scarf the ends the same as for a flat weld, taking care to have the scarfs come on opposite sides of the stock, as shown at 2.

STEP THREE.—Heat the piece, and bend it into shape in the same manner as the ring of Exercise 1.

STEP FOUR.—Bring the scarfs tightly together, as at 4.

STEP FIVE.—Heat the scarfs slowly, to prevent the outer one from burning before the inner one is hot enough to weld. Weld the ring over the horn of the anvil, and finish it with a flatter. It should then be heated uniformly thruout, and rounded on a cone. In order to prevent it from becoming tapered while doing this, it must be reversed on the cone and expanded equally from both sides.

Bolts are made in three different ways, *i. e.,* by forging, upsetting, or welding. The first of these methods is ordinarily used for special bolts and those that are to be finished or turned to size. Such bolts are forged from stock having a diameter equal to that of the head, and are therefore the stongest kind made. The second method, in which the stock is upset to form the head, is the one most commonly used for both hand- and machine-made bolts. In the third method the head is formed by welding a ring of stock around the stem. If equally well made, an upset-head bolt is stronger than a welded-head bolt.

The size of a bolt is given by the diameter and length of the shank. Thus a 1 x 12-inch bolt means one with a shank 1

BAND RING

Stock: $\frac{1}{4}$" × $1\frac{1}{4}$" × $13\frac{7}{8}$" Wrot Iron

inch in diameter and 12 inches long from the under side of the head to the end. The dimensions of a bolt-head are governed by the diameter of the shank, and are entirely independent of the length. For square and hexagonal bolt-heads, the distance across the flats is equal to $1\frac{1}{2}$ times the diameter of the shank plus $\frac{1}{8}$ inch, and the thickness of the head is equal to the diameter of the shank. Thus a 1-inch bolt should have a head $1\frac{1}{2} \times 1 + \frac{1}{8}$, or $1\frac{5}{8}$ inches across the flats, and 1 inch thick. These are the dimensions for rough heads, each dimension for a finished head being $\frac{1}{16}$ inch less than for a rough head.

Heading-Tool.—For squaring-up the under side of the head on a bolt, a heading-tool (Fig. 36) is required. In use this is placed on the face of the anvil, so that while the head of the bolt is being forged the shank can project down thru the heading-tool and the hardie-hole. The hole in this tool should be slightly larger than the stock for which it is intended, in order that a shank, when heated, may drop thru it easily. For this reason a different heading-tool is required for each size of round stock used.

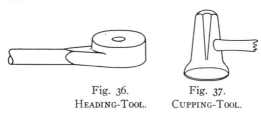

Fig. 36.
HEADING-TOOL.

Fig. 37.
CUPPING-TOOL.

Cupping-Tool.—Bolt heads generally have the top corners rounded, or chamfered. This is ordinarily done with a cupping-tool (Fig. 37), but a top-swage, or a hand-hammer may be used.

Exercise 17. Upset-Head Bolt. (Plate XVII.)

STEP ONE.—Cut the stock to length, and square both ends. Heat one end for about 2 inches to a yellow heat. Place the

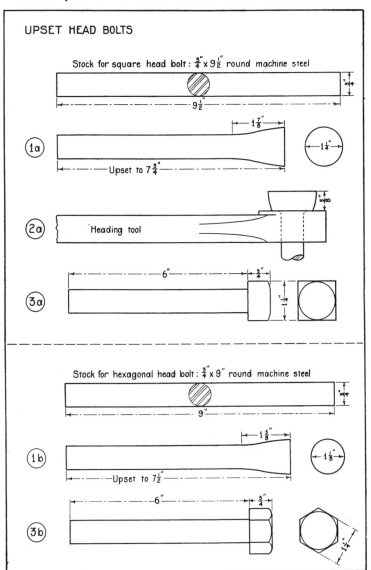

UPSET HEAD BOLTS

Stock for square head bolt: ¾″ x 9½″ round machine steel

9½″
¾″

1a — Upset to 7¾″ — 1⅞″ — 1¼″

2a — Heading tool — ½″

3a — 6″ — ¾″ — 1¼″

Stock for hexagonal head bolt: ¾″ x 9″ round machine steel

9″
¾″

1b — Upset to 7½″ — 1⅝″ — 1⅛″

3b — 6″ — ¾″ — 1¼″

hot end on the face of the anvil, holding the piece vertical with a pair of link-tongs, and strike on the cold end with a heavy hand-hammer. Care should be taken to keep the stock straight while upsetting.

STEP TWO.—Bring the upset end to a high heat, and insert the shank in a heading-tool. Form the head by flattening the upset portion, as shown at 2. To aid in keeping the shank at the center of the head, a circle with a radius about ½ inch greater than that of the hole should be drawn with chalk on the face of the tool. The student can then tell when one side of the head is out too far.

STEP THREE.—Forge the head square or hexagonal on the face of the anvil. Insert the shank in a heading-tool and chamfer the top corners with a cupping-tool. The shank should be finished between top- and bottom-swages.

Exercise 18. Welded-Head Bolt. (Plate XVIII.)

STEP ONE.—If a piece of stock the required size is not available, draw-out a large piece to the size shown at 1.

STEP TWO.—Cut off the end at an angle on the hardie, and make another cut half-way thru the stock at the point indicated.

STEP THREE.—Bend the drawn-out portion over the horn as shown at 3.

STEP FOUR.—Break off the bent portion, and finish the bending over a piece of cold ¾-inch round stock. This collar should then be hammered approximately square, and made to appear as shown at 4. If it were made round, the joint might show on one side when finished, making a poor appearing head.

STEP FIVE.—Bring one end of the shank to a welding heat, and upset it in the cold collar, as at 5. Before starting to weld it be sure that the shank will slip thru the heading-tool.

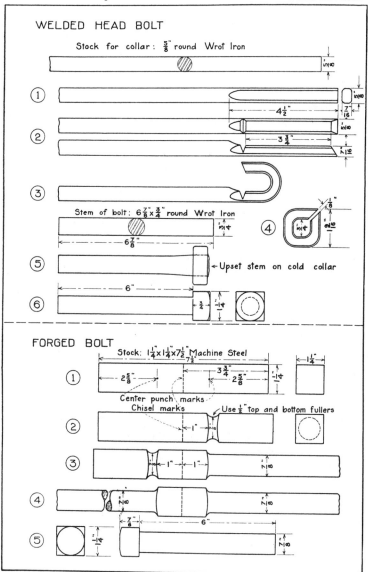

WELDED HEAD BOLT

Stock for collar: $\frac{5}{8}$" round Wrot Iron

① $4\frac{1}{2}$"

② $3\frac{3}{4}$"

③

Stem of bolt: $6\frac{7}{8}$" x $\frac{3}{4}$" round Wrot Iron

④

$6\frac{7}{8}$"

⑤ ←Upset stem on cold collar

⑥ 6"

FORGED BOLT

Stock: $1\frac{1}{4}$" x $1\frac{1}{4}$" x $7\frac{1}{2}$" Machine Steel

① $7\frac{1}{2}$" $2\frac{5}{8}$" $3\frac{3}{4}$" $2\frac{5}{8}$" $1\frac{1}{4}$"

Center punch marks
Chisel marks

② Use $\frac{1}{2}$" top and bottom fullers 1"

③ 1" 1"

④ $\frac{7}{8}$" $\frac{7}{8}$"

⑤ $\frac{7}{8}$" 6" $\frac{7}{8}$"

STEP SIX.—Heat the head slowly, to prevent the collar from burning, and weld it by hammering on all four sides. Finish it in a heading-tool in the same manner as an upset head.

If there is too much stock on the bolt head, forge it to the proper size across the flats, and cut the surplus stock off of the end with a hot eye-chisel.

Exercise 19. Forged Bolt. (Plate XVIII.)

It is necessary for two students to work together on this exercise, so a piece of stock long enough to make two bolts should be used.

STEP ONE.—Cut the stock to length, and mark it with a center-punch and a chisel as indicated.

STEP TWO.—Fuller one end, as shown at 2.

STEP THREE.—Draw-out the end A to size under a trip-hammer.

STEP FOUR.—Fuller and hammer out the other end in the same manner.

STEP FIVE.—Cut the stock thru the center along the dotted line. Reheat, and insert the shank of one end in a heading-tool, finishing the head in the same manner as the upset head.

The shank and under side of the head of a forged bolt are generally turned to the finished size in the machine shop. In some cases, however, such bolts are forged to the required sizes, so that no machine work is necessary.

CHAPTER IV.

Special Welds.

The **Butt Weld** is made by rounding the ends of two pieces of stock and driving them together at a welding heat, as shown in Fig. 38. The purpose in rounding the ends is to permit squeezing the molten oxide out of the joint. If they were concave, impurities would be held between the two pieces, making an unsound weld.

When the pieces of stock are short the butting, or welding, is generally done on the anvil, but with long pieces it is done in the fire. Long pieces are placed end to end in the fire, and when the welding heat has been reached they are driven together. In doing this the blacksmith holds one of them to steady it, while the helper strikes on the projecting end of the other. When the pieces are stuck together the resulting bar is removed from the fire, and hammered to size on the anvil. It is then smoothed between top- and bottom-swages.

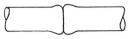

Fig. 38. Butt-Weld.

A butt weld may be used on $1\frac{1}{4}$-inch stock or larger. It is not as safe or as strong as a lap weld, but has the advantage of requiring no upsetting and scarfing of ends. All the upsetting necessary occurs during the welding process.

V-Weld.—Another weld suitable for large-sized stock is the V-weld. The ends of the stock are first cut with a hot chisel to the form shown in Fig. 39. The pieces are then placed end to end in the fire and heated. The square end of the short, chisel-pointed piece should project over the edge of the forge. When the stock is at the welding heat, this end is struck with a backing-hammer or a sledge, depending on the size of the stock. This upsets and welds the ends together. The joint is then hammered to size and swaged on the anvil.

The V-weld is suitable for welding round or square steel and wrought iron. Besides being easy to make, on account of the elimination of upsetting and scarfing, it forms an ex-

Fig. 39. V-WELD.

tremely strong joint. It is not suitable for stock less than $1\frac{1}{2}$ inches in diameter, as smaller stock bends while the pieces are being driven together in the fire.

The **Jump-Weld** is one ordinarily used by shipsmiths on marine or ship work. Its applications are numerous, but its main principle is the joining of one end of round, square, or rectangular stock to some point on the side of a piece of stock of the same or of a different size.

In making the "jump," shown at *A* in Fig. 40, the end of the stock is brought to the welding heat and hammered on the

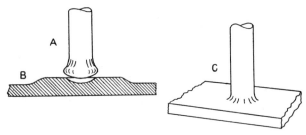

Fig. 40. JUMP WELD.

sides, to prevent it from bursting while scarfing it. If the piece is a short one, the scarfing may be done by standing it on end on the anvil and hammering the hot end so as to form a flange, similar to the one shown at *A*.

If this piece is to be "jumped," or welded, to a piece of flat stock, the latter must be made thicker where the joint is to be, in order to allow for hammering. This can be done either by upsetting the flat stock or by forging it from a thicker piece. An indentation is made at this point with a bob-punch, as shown at *B,* to accommodate the flanged end on the "jump."

The two pieces are generally brought to the welding heat in separate fires. The flat piece is then placed on the anvil and the "jump" in position on it. The end of the "jump" is struck with a sledge, and the flange quickly welded down with a top-fuller, making the joint appear as shown at *C,* Fig. 40.

The **Split-Weld** is used for welding together the ends of thin stock, such as brake-bands and sheet steel. If an ordinary lap-weld were used for this purpose, the time lost in getting the scarfed ends in position for welding would permit thin stock to cool, making welding difficult. With the split-

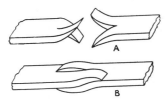

Fig. 41. SPLIT-WELD.

weld the scarfs are in position when placed on the anvil, and may be hammered together immediately.

The ends of the pieces to be joined are upset and scarfed or tapered to a blunt edge. They are then split down the center, as shown at *A,* Fig. 41, for a distance depending on the thickness of the stock, but ordinarily about ¾ inch. One-half of each end is bent up and the other half down, as at *A.* The ends are then heated, pushed tightly together, and closed down on each other, as shown at B in Fig. 41. The welding is done in the regular way.

Split-Weld for Heavy Stock.—A split-weld suitable for heavy stock is shown in Fig. 42. In making this weld the ends of the pieces are upset and scarfed, as at A, one end

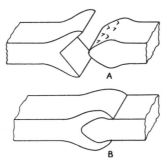

Fig. 42.   SPLIT-WELD FOR HEAVY STOCK.

being pointed and the other split and shaped like a Y. The pieces are then driven together and closed down, one on the other, ready for welding, as shown at B, Fig. 42.

This weld, or one very similar to it, is often used when

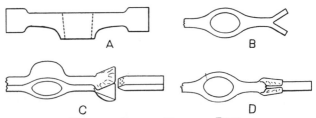

Fig. 43.   WELDING TIP ON A PICK.

welding tool steel to iron or to machinery steel. An example of this is the "steeling" of the Norway iron body of a pick, shown at A, Fig. 43. The ends of this body are split and shaped as shown at B. The piece to be welded on is ·about $\frac{1}{2}$ x 1 inch and from 4 to 5 inches long. It is pointed and notched with a chisel, as at C, to prevent it from falling out while heating. The two pieces are then driven together and the ends of the Y closed down, as shown at D. They are heated slowly, to prevent the tool steel from being burned, and welded under a trip-hammer or with a sledge. The end of the pick is drawn to a point under the trip-hammer, and made smooth with a flatter. It is then reheated, hardened, and the temper color drawn to a dark blue.

Exercise 20. T-Weld. (Plate XIX.)

STEP ONE.—Cut off a piece of stock for the leg of the T, and upset it as shown.

STEP TWO.—Start the scarf with the hand-hammer, as at 2.

STEP THREE.—Bring the scarf to the form shown at 3 with a ½-inch top-fuller.

STEP FOUR.—Finish this scarf with the same fuller, then smooth it with a hand-hammer.

STEP FIVE.—Upset the cross-piece at the center, as shown at 5.

STEP SIX.—Form the scarf as at 6 with the bob-punch of Fig. 16. This can be done by using the peen of a hand-hammer and striking on its face with a heavier hammer; but it is rather dangerous, as the face of the hand-hammer is liable to break unless the heavier hammer is wielded by an expert.

STEP SEVEN.—Bring the scarfed portions of the two pieces to the welding heat and weld them, using a hammer to stick them together and a necking-tool or fuller to weld down the edges of the scarf. In removing the pieces from the fire for welding, the cross-piece should be taken in the right hand and the other piece in the left. This leaves the right hand free for hammering after the pieces have been placed in position. A student should practice putting the pieces together while cold, before attempting to weld them.

After the welding has been finished the stock should be smoothed between top- and bottom-swages, and the scale removed with a file. The ends are then trimmed off, making the dimensions of the T as shown at 7.

With flat stock the scarfs for a T-weld are made in the same manner.

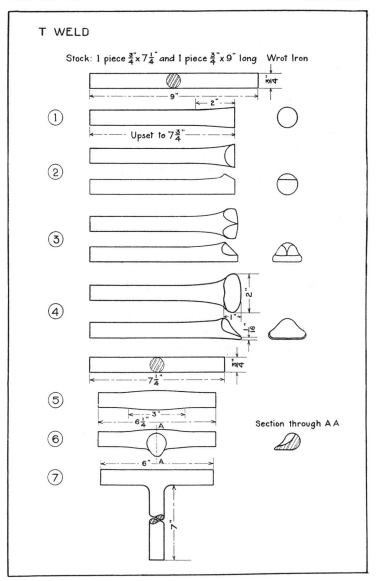

T WELD

Stock: 1 piece $\frac{3}{4}$" x $7\frac{1}{4}$" and 1 piece $\frac{3}{4}$" x 9" long   Wrot Iron

Exercise 21. Angle Weld. (Plate XX.)

STEP ONE.—Cut and upset the short piece for the angle to the size shown at 1. Since the stock has to be upset for a considerable distance from the end, the tip should be partially cooled in water, to prevent the upsetting from taking place mostly at that point.

STEP TWO.—Scarf this piece with a bob-punch or the peen of a hammer, as shown at 2. The length of this scarf should be slightly less than the width of the one on the other piece, so that the lip A (4) will lap over on the thick portion of the stock.

STEP THREE.—Cut and upset the other piece to the form shown at 3.

STEP FOUR.—Start the scarf on this piece in the same manner as for the flat lap-weld. It should, however, be allowed to widen out, in order to furnish material for the lip A, which is made by placing the stock on edge on the anvil with the scarf projecting over the rounded edge and hitting the upper edge with a hand-hammer. The top edge should then appear straight, as shown.

STEP FIVE.—After bringing the two scarfed ends to a welding heat remove the pieces from the fire, holding the short one (2) in the right hand and the long one (4) in the left. Weld the joint with a heavy hand-hammer, and finish it with a flatter. The scale should then be removed with a file, and the ends cut off to length with a hot chisel.

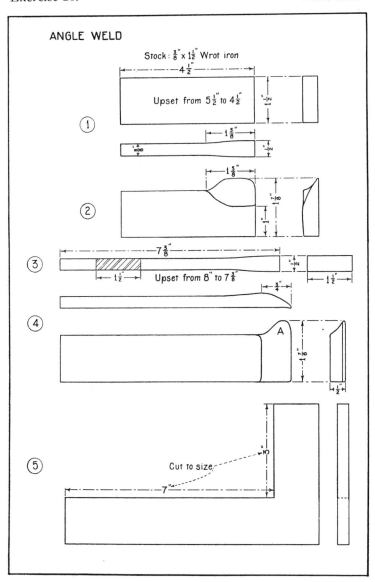

ANGLE WELD

Stock: ⅜" x 1½" Wrot iron

① Upset from 5½" to 4½"

②

③ Upset from 8" to 7⅜"

④ A

⑤ Cut to size

CHAPTER V.

HAMMER WORK.

In making forgings larger than the exercises previously described in this book, some type of power hammer is invariably used. Those commonly found in technical schools are the trip- or belt-hammer and the steam-hammer.

The **Trip-** or **Belt-Hammer** (Fig. 44) is used for hammering medium or small-sized forgings. Its size is designated by the weight of the falling parts, *i. e.,* in a 125-pound hammer the combined weight of the falling parts is 125 pounds.

The frame of the machine surrounds the anvil, or die block, *B,* but the two are usually mounted on separate foundations. This is done so that the continual use of the hammer will not have a tendency to break the frame, and also in order to permit adjustment of the position of the lower die.

This type of hammer is belt driven, the blows being regulated by means of the foot-treadle, *T.* This gives very good control of the hammer except at starting, when the blows are sometimes rather jerky. As hammering continues the blows become more uniform. A student should receive special instructions in the manipulation of a trip-hammer before starting to use it.

When drawing-out stock with a trip-hammer the material should be placed at the center of the dies. If it is placed at one side there will be an undue stress on the springs, and they will be likely to break.

Hollow-bit tongs are generally used for holding work at the power-hammer, as a firm grip can be obtained with them on either round, square, or flat material. Flat-jawed tongs should not be used, as they give a very poor grip when the jaws are in the vertical position. To maintain a firm grip, a link should be slipped over the handles of the tongs, so as to hold them close together.

A trip-hammer may also be employed for making drop forgings by using special dies that may be made of cast iron.

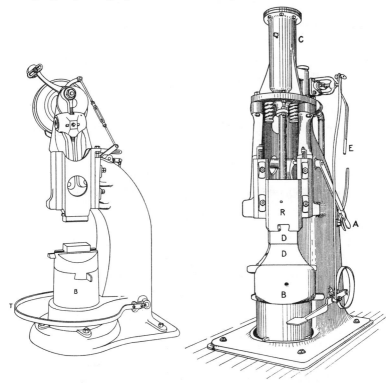

Fig. 44. TRIP-HAMMER.   Fig. 45. STEAM-HAMMER.

This type of hammer has the advantage over a steam-hammer in the matter of lower first cost and great economy in operation. It is not, however, so well suited to very heavy work.

The **Steam-Hammer** is generally made in larger sizes than

the trip-hammer, the combined weight of the falling parts ranging from a few hundred to several thousand pounds. A 500-pound hammer is shown in Fig. 45.

As the name implies, this hammer is driven by steam. The latter enters at the top of the cylinder, C, and forces down the ram, R. The blow is controlled and regulated by means of the levers, A and E, which are operated by an assistant. If the blacksmith works alone, the hammer may be controlled by means of the foot-treadle.

The ram, R, and the dies, D, are generally placed at an angle of 45° with the front of the frame. This permits the hammering of material either across or lengthwise on the die without interference. As with the trip-hammer, the die-block, B, rests on a separate foundation from that of the frame.

Finishing Allowance.—Forgings made under a hammer are often machined or finished to size. For this reason a certain allowance should be made for finishing them. The amount of this allowance varies from ⅛ inch on small forgings to ¾ inch on large ones. Take as an example a shaft which is to be finished 8 inches in diameter. It should be forged to a diameter of from 8½ to 8¾ inches.

Exercise 22. Forged Open-End Wrench. (Plate XXI.)

When making this exercise it is necessary for two students to work together, as it is inconvenient to make such a wrench alone. Considerable time will also be saved in this way.

STEP ONE.—Cut off a piece of machine steel to the size indicated, and mark it with a center-punch, as shown at 1. A piece 4⅜ inches long would be enough to make this wrench, but it would be hard to hold while being worked under a trip-hammer, as the tongs would become hot and afford a poor grip. There should be enough of a tong hold to prevent

FORGED OPEN END WRENCH

Stock: $\frac{5}{8}$" x $1\frac{3}{4}$" x $9\frac{1}{2}$" machine steel

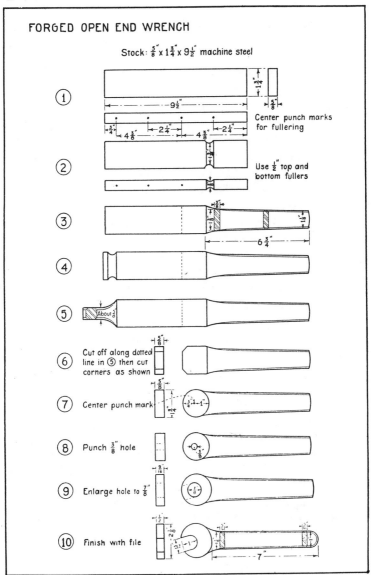

①

② Use $\frac{1}{2}$" top and bottom fullers

Center punch marks for fulling

③

④

⑤

⑥ Cut off along dotted line in ⑤ then cut corners as shown

⑦ Center punch mark

⑧ Punch $\frac{3}{8}$" hole

⑨ Enlarge hole to $\frac{7}{8}$"

⑩ Finish with file

the jaws of the tongs from being caught between the dies. It is therefore best to use a piece of stock 9½ inches long. This will give enough material for two wrenches, with an allowance for a short tong hold. Remember to use hollow-bit tongs. Flat-jawed tongs are unsafe.

STEP TWO.—Use ½-inch top- and bottom-fullers to make the grooves shown at 2. To insure uniformity in the depth of these marks the stock should be turned over several times when fullering.

STEP THREE.—Draw-out the handle under the trip-hammer, leaving it wider than the finished size, to allow for swaging the edges.

STEP FOUR.—Use ½-inch top- and bottom-fullers on the other end, as shown at 4.

STEP FIVE.—Draw-out this end to provide for a tong hold when making the second wrench.

STEP SIX.—Cut off the stock with a hot chisel along the dotted line shown at 5. The corners should then be cut off, to facilitate rounding the head.

STEP SEVEN.—Round the head by placing it on a 1¾-inch bottom-swage and using a 1-inch top-fuller on the neck or fillet. A set-hammer or a ¼-inch top-fuller can be used for rounding the circular part adjacent to the handle. Finish shaping with a hand-hammer, leaving the head ⅝ inch thick.

STEP EIGHT.—Punch a ⅜-inch hole thru the head at the center-punch mark shown at 7.

STEP NINE.—Enlarge this hole to ⅞-inch diameter by driving in a drift-pin. If when doing this the stock becomes thinner at one side, that side should be cooled before enlarging the hole further. This equalizes the thickness of the stock around the hole. Thin the head with a flatter to 9⁄16 inch.

STEP TEN.—Place a suitable sheet-iron template on top of the exercise, and mark with a cold chisel the lines for the opening in the head, as shown by the dotted lines at 9. These marks should make an angle of 15° with the handle of the wrench. The opening in the head is then cut with a hot chisel and the head hammered so as to make it ½ inch thick.

Square the inside of the jaws on a saddle, as shown in Fig. 46. If the ends are too long they should be cut to the

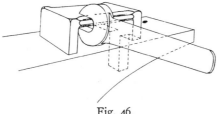

Fig. 46.

correct length on the saddle, in order to prevent them from becoming too thin.

Finish the edges of the handle between ½-inch top- and bottom-swages and the faces with a flatter. After the wrench has cooled the inside of the jaws should be filed to fit a nut. The wrench is then case-hardened, as described in Chapter VI.

Exercise 23. Flat-Jawed Tongs. (Plates XXII – XXIII.)

STEP ONE.—Cut a piece of machine steel for the jaws, and mark it as shown at 1.

STEP TWO.—Heat one end and place it on the anvil with the center-punch mark at the rounded edge, as shown in Fig. A. Hammer it as indicated, gradually raising the cold end until it is parallel with the face of the anvil, as shown by the dotted lines. This forms the shoulder, shown at 2. If the stock were held flat on the anvil when starting this shoulder, it would probably move forward after each blow, thus making the shoulder a poor one.

STEP THREE.—Give the stock a quarter turn to the left, and place it on the anvil as shown in Fig. B. Hammer out the stock for the eye, taking care to have the blows fall directly above the edge of the anvil. This is done to prevent the jaw from bending upward while hammering.

When placing the stock on the anvil for hammering the eye, it should never be turned to the right. This would make the tongs left-handed. In the finished tongs the handle of the top jaw should look toward the right.

STEP FOUR.—With a ½-inch top- or bottom-fuller make a mark as shown at 4. Form the second jaw on the other end of the stock in the same manner. The stock should then be cut through the center at the chisel mark, as shown at 4 in Plate XXIV.

STEP FIVE.—Draw-out the stub end (to which the handle is to be welded) on the anvil, and scarf it, as shown at 5. Several cuts should be made on the face of the scarf with a hardie, to prevent the pieces from slipping apart when welding.

STEP SIX.—Cut a piece of stock long enough to make both handles, and upset it at the ends, as shown at 6.

STEP SEVEN.—Scarf the ends of this piece as shown. If this stock is also of machine steel, the scarfs must be nicked in the same manner as those on the jaws.

STEP EIGHT.—Weld the jaws on the ends of this piece, then cut it at the center. Finish the portion of the handle near the eye with a flatter. Round the eye on the horn of the anvil with a ½-inch top-fuller, as shown in Fig. C. Finish hammering the jaw to size, and make a groove thru the center with a ⅜-inch top-fuller. This groove enables one to hold round stock with these tongs. It also insures a better grip on

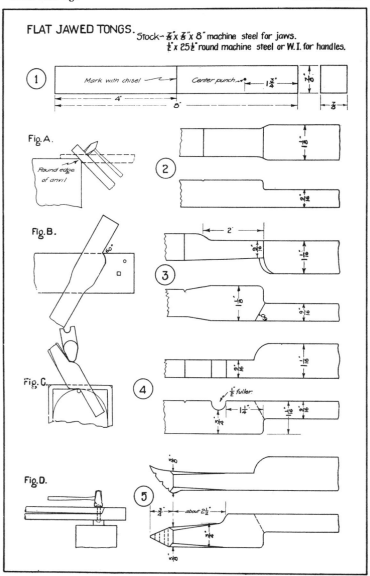

FLAT JAWED TONGS. Stock—$\frac{5}{8}$"x $\frac{5}{8}$"x 8" machine steel for jaws.
$\frac{1}{2}$"x 25$\frac{1}{2}$" round machine steel or W.I. for handles.

(1) Mark with chisel →   Center punch →   1$\frac{3}{4}$" $\frac{7}{8}$"
     ←— 4" —→
     ←————— 8" —————→ $\frac{5}{8}$"

Fig. A.   Round edge of anvil

(2)   1$\frac{1}{8}$"
       2$\frac{1}{4}$"

Fig. B.   60°

(3) ←— 2" —→
     0$\frac{1}{2}$"   1$\frac{1}{16}$"
     1$\frac{1}{8}$" $\frac{9}{16}$"

Fig. C.

(4) $\frac{9}{16}$"   1$\frac{1}{8}$"
     ←$\frac{1}{2}$" fuller
     1$\frac{3}{4}$"   1$\frac{1}{4}$"   1$\frac{1}{16}$"   2$\frac{3}{4}$"

Fig. D.

(5) $\frac{5}{10}$"
     $\frac{3}{4}$"   ←— about 2$\frac{1}{2}$" —→
     $\frac{5}{10}$" $\frac{5}{10}$"

flat material, since both sides of the jaws grip firmly. Without the groove the jaws might touch the stock at the center only. A series of cross cuts, as shown, should be made with a hot chisel, to produce a still firmer hold.

STEP NINE.—Punch the rivet hole shown at 9 so that a ⅜-inch rivet will easily drop into the hole. Bring the straight end of the rivet to a high heat and insert it in the holes in the two eyes. Turn the tongs over and place the rivet head on a bottom snap as shown in Fig. D. Head the heated end of the rivet by first giving it a few blows with the face of a hand-hammer, then rounding it with the peen of the hammer, and finally smoothing it with the top snap, or riveting tool.

After riveting, the tongs will be stiff and will not open. This should be remedied by heating them at the rivet and opening and shutting them several times. Finish the tongs by fitting them to the stock on which they are to be used.

Exercise 24. Link Tongs. (Plates XXIV – XXV.)

STEPS ONE TO SEVEN are the same as for the flat-jawed tongs.

STEP EIGHT.—Weld on the handles in the same manner as before. Draw-out the jaws, and finish them with a flatter to the form shown at 8. Cut off their ends with a hardie, as shown.

STEP NINE.—Punch the holes for a ⅜-inch rivet, and bend the ends of the jaws over the rounded edge of the anvil to the form at 9.

STEP TEN.—Finish bending the jaws over the horn of the anvil. This bending may also be done with a bottom-swage and a top-fuller.

STEP ELEVEN.—Rivet the parts together, and finish the tongs in the same manner as the flat-jawed tongs.

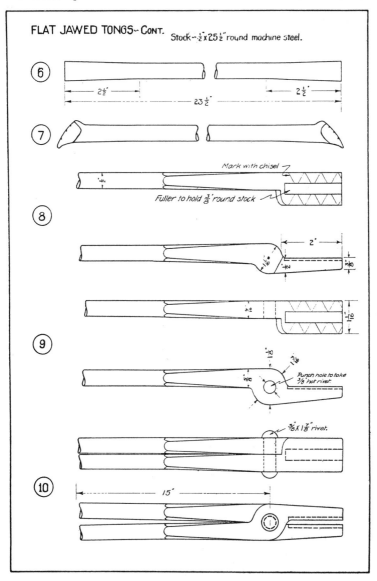

FLAT JAWED TONGS – CONT. Stock – ½″ x 25½″ round machine steel.

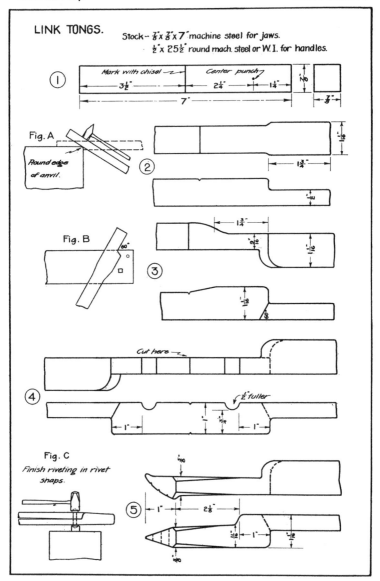

LINK TONGS. Stock – $\frac{7}{8}$" x $\frac{7}{8}$" x 7" machine steel for jaws.
$\frac{1}{2}$" x 25$\frac{1}{2}$" round mach. steel or W.I. for handles.

① Mark with chisel — Center punch — $\frac{7}{8}$" $\frac{7}{8}$"

3$\frac{1}{2}$" — 2$\frac{1}{4}$" — 1$\frac{1}{4}$" — 7"

Fig. A

Round edge of anvil.

② 1$\frac{1}{16}$" 1$\frac{3}{4}$" $\frac{1}{2}$"

Fig. B 60°

③ 1$\frac{3}{4}$" $\frac{9}{16}$" 1$\frac{1}{16}$" 1$\frac{1}{16}$" 60°

④ Cut here — $\frac{1}{4}$" fuller

1" $\frac{3}{4}$" 1"

Fig. C

Finish riveting in rivet snaps.

⑤ $\frac{1}{10}$" 1" 2$\frac{1}{8}$"

$\frac{1}{10}$" 1$\frac{1}{16}$" 1" 1$\frac{1}{16}$"

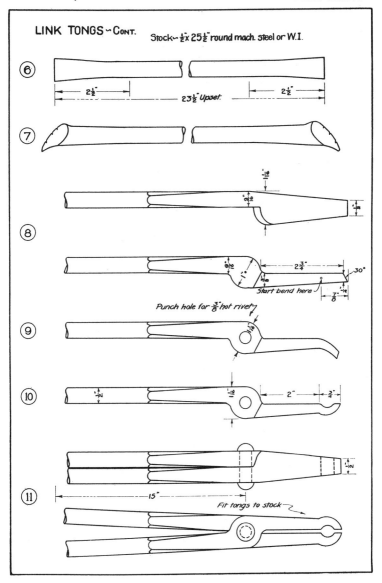

LINK TONGS ~ Cont.   Stock ~ ½" x 25½" round mach. steel or W.I.

Exercise 25.   Hollow-Bit Tongs.   (Plate XXVI.)

One of the methods used for making hollow-bit tongs is shown in Plate XXVI. A student who has made the majority of the preceding exercises should be able to make a pair of these tongs without a detailed explanation of the various steps. However, the following points should be noted:

At 3 the stock for the jaw is shown fullered and ready for shaping to size. It should be flattened and brought to the desired form with a square-edge set-hammer. The object of the fuller marks is to leave the neck thick, thereby making a stronger jaw.

Enough stock is provided in this exercise for drawing-out the handles. This is done under the trip-hammer. The handles are then rounded between top- and bottom-swages.

The flat end, or jaw proper, is bent to the form at 5 by placing it on a V-block and using a top-fuller on the inside, as shown in Fig. A.

To bend the stock between the jaw proper and the eye to the form shown at 7, place it over the rounded edge of the anvil and use a 1-inch top-fuller on it, as shown in Fig. B.

After riveting the tongs, they should be fitted to a piece of square stock of the size on which they are to be used.

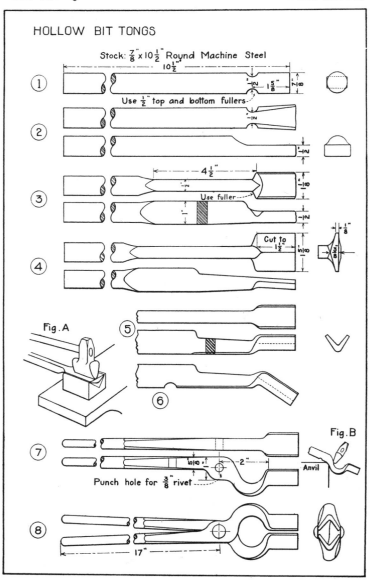

HOLLOW BIT TONGS

Stock: $\frac{7}{8}$" x $10\frac{1}{2}$" Round Machine Steel

① $10\frac{1}{2}$" — Use $\frac{1}{2}$" top and bottom fullers — $1\frac{5}{8}$" — $\frac{7}{8}$" — $\frac{1}{2}$"

②

$1\frac{1}{2}$"

③ $4\frac{1}{2}$" — Use fuller — $1\frac{1}{8}$" — $\frac{1}{2}$" — $\frac{1}{2}$" — $\frac{1}{2}$"

④ Cut to $1\frac{1}{2}$ — $1\frac{5}{8}$" — $\frac{1}{8}$" — $\frac{3}{16}$"

Fig. A

⑤

⑥

⑦ Punch hole for $\frac{3}{8}$" rivet — $\frac{5}{8}$" — 2" — Fig. B — Anvil

⑧ 17"

CHAPTER VI.

Annealing, Hardening and Tempering Steel.

Annealing.—When carbon steel is heated to a temperature of about 1400° F. and allowed to cool slowly, it becomes soft, or annealed. The more slowly it is cooled the softer it is when cold.

There are two objects in annealing: first, to soften the metal, and second, to remove internal stresses. For instance, a piece of tool steel is generally softened or annealed before being worked in a lathe or otherwise machined.

The common method of annealing tool steel is to heat it to a cherry-red and bury it in ashes or slaked lime until it has entirely cooled. Care must be taken not to heat the steel too much, or its grain will become coarse and the steel weakened. The ashes and lime used should be perfectly dry, so that they will be poor conductors of heat and cause the steel to cool slowly.

Box Annealing.—In annealing a large number of steel pieces, they are usually packed with ground bone or fine charcoal in cast-iron boxes and placed in an annealing furnace. When they have reached the proper temperature the draft is shut off, and the furnace is allowed to cool slowly. The steel is not removed from the boxes until it is cold.

This method of annealing prevents the steel from being covered with scale, because no air is admitted and the oxygen of the air in the boxes is consumed by the red-hot carbon.

Water Annealing.—The quickest method of annealing steel is known as "water annealing." It will not leave the steel as soft as when cooled slowly in lime or ashes, but it often serves the purpose more conveniently. A case in which this would be so is when a drill or tap has broken off in a piece of work and must be softened before it can be removed

The procedure is to heat the steel to a dull red and plunge it in water. Soapy water gives very good results for this purpose.

Hardening.—If instead of allowing steel to cool slowly from a cherry-red heat it is cooled suddenly, it will become very hard. The hardness will depend upon the percentage of carbon in the steel, the temperature at which it is hardened, and the speed with which it is cooled. The following two laws of hardening should be borne in mind while hardening tool steel:

1. The higher the percentage of carbon in the steel the lower will be the refining, or hardening, heat.

2. The more quickly steel is cooled from the hardening heat the harder it becomes.

From these laws it follows that the hardness of any piece of steel may be varied by varying the rate of cooling.

Refining Heat.—The only way to determine the proper heat at which a piece of tool steel should be hardened is by experimenting in the following manner: Draw-out a sample of the steel into a bar about ⅜ inch square. One end of this bar is heated to a dull-red and quickly cooled in water having a temperature of about 70° F. When cold it is placed on the anvil with about 1 inch of this end projecting over the rounded edge. An attempt is then made to break off this projecting end by hitting it with a hand-hammer. If it bends, the temperature at which it was hardened was not high enough. This test should then be repeated, raising the temperature slightly each time until the steel, when cooled, will be file-hard, i. e., a file will not cut it; will not break easily; and will have a fine grain. If the temperature is raised too high the grain of the steel will be coarse, showing large crystals. The steel will also be very brittle, not so strong, and will not hold a cutting edge well.

The refining heat may then be defined as the temperature which gives the steel, when hardened, the finest grain, leaves it file-hard, and also leaves it in the strongest condition.

Recalescence.—When steel is heated to a bright-red heat and allowed to cool, the rate of cooling is not uniform. It will cool gradually until a certain temperature is reached, when it will seem to become hotter for a short time and the color lighter. Below this temperature the cooling is gradual again.

The temperature at which this apparent re-heating occurs is the proper refining or hardening heat for the steel tested. It can be determined by the use of a Pyrometer. This phenomenon is known as "recalescence." In water annealing, the hard steel should be heated to somewhat below this temperature.

Tempering.—After tools have been hardened in the manner described above, they are too hard and brittle for most purposes, and must be softened a little. This process of slightly softening the hardened steel is known as "drawing the temper," or properly "tempering."

Tempering is accomplished by reheating the hardened steel, and quickly cooling it again, the amount of the reheating depending upon the use for which the tool is intended. The accompanying chart gives the approximate temperatures at which various tools are tempered. Thus if a piece of hardened tool steel is heated to a temperature of about $430°$ F. it will be only slightly softened, and will still be hard enough for small lathe tools.

These temperatures can be determined in several ways. If the hardening and tempering is done on a large scale, an oil bath may be used. Such a bath is maintained at the desired temperature as indicated by a thermometer, and the steel placed in it after being hardened. When the steel has reached the same temperature as the bath, it is removed and quickly cooled.

For ordinary purposes the temperature is gauged by the

GUIDE FOR HARDENING AND TEMPERING
CARBON TOOL STEEL

APPLICATIONS	TEMPER-ATURE	COLOR OF OXIDE	ACTION OF FILE
Engraving tools, lathe tools, and tools for cutting hard metals at slow speed.	430°	Very pale yellow	File will hardly mark
Lathe and planer tools for heavy work, milling cutters, taps, reamers, thread-cutting tools, punches, dies, etc.	460°	Straw yellow	File will mark
Various punches and dies, wood-working tools, twist drills, sledges, blacksmith's hand-hammers, stone drills, etc.	500°	Deep straw (or brown-yellow)	File will mark a little deeper
Shear knives, rivet snaps, punches, boilermakers' tools, and cold chisels for light work.	525°	Light purple	
Cold chisels for ordinary work, gears, surgical instruments, etc.	570°	Blue tinged with red	Files, but with difficulty
Springs, picks, etc.	580°	Blue	
	625° to 650°	Gray or green	

color of oxide on the steel. This film of oxide forms on the polished surface of steel if heat is applied. It is first visible at a temperature of about 430°, when the color is a very pale yellow. As the temperature rises, the color changes from pale yellow to dark yellow, to brown, then to light purple, to dark purple, and finally to blue. These colors serve as a guide for tempering. After the metal has been cooled they remain visible, indicating the last temperature to which it was heated. Common iron shows this same phenomenon.

Up to a visible red heat, the higher the temperature of reheating the softer the steel becomes. If the steel is reheated to too high a temperature it must be rehardened and tempered again.

The best shop method for testing the hardness of a tool is to try it with a file. The action of a file on steel which has been tempered at the different colors is given in the chart; but while this method may indicate that a tool has the proper hardness, the grain may be coarse because of too high a hardening heat. This last condition gives the tool a crumbly and scratchy cutting edge.

Tempering Only the Cutting Edges of Tools.—Certain tools are tempered only at the cutting edges, the main body being left unhardened in order to resist shocks. They are all tempered in the same manner, the only difference being in the final hardness of the cutting edge. The tempering of a chisel will serve as an example of the process employed.

After the chisel has been forged, it should be allowed to cool until black, and then reheated for hardening about 3 inches back from the edge. When reheating, the cutting edge should be kept high in the fire, so that the heat will be applied to the thick part of the chisel and flow toward the cutting edge. The chisel should be kept well covered with coke, and heated slowly.

The hardening is done by quick cooling in water at a temperature of about 70° F. This water should be clean, since dirty water retards cooling. The chisel is held vertically, and the cutting edge gradually inserted in the water until about half of the heated portion is below the surface. The tool must be moved around while doing this, so that the steam generated will not blow the water away and retard the cooling. It should never be held stationary in the water, since if there is a well-defined line between the cooled and hot portions the chisel will probably break at that point. The chisel is then quickly plunged into the water and immediately removed, considerable heat remaining in it but the edge being cold.

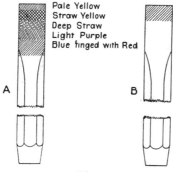

Pale Yellow
Straw Yellow
Deep Straw
Light Purple
Blue finged with Red

A

B

Fig. 47.

For the purpose of watching the colors, the cutting end is polished with a carborundum stone or a piece of emery cloth. These temper colors will first appear next to the heated portion of the chisel when the heat from that part runs down into the point. They will move down toward the point in the order shown at *A* in Fig. 47. When the color at the cutting edge is blue tinged with red, as at *B*, the tool is completely cooled to prevent further reheating and softening of the point.

A lathe tool is hardened and tempered in the same manner, except that the final cooling is done when the yellow scale appears at the cutting edge.

Hardening and Tempering Tools Thruout.—When a tool is to be tempered thruout it is first heated uniformly to the refining heat, and then completely cooled. After removing it from the cooling bath it is dried, and the surface polished. It is tempered by laying it on a piece of red-hot iron until the desired color appears on the polished surface, when it is again cooled in water or oil. The tool should be turned frequently, in order to have the heating take place uniformly. If this is not done the parts in contact with the hot iron will become overheated and too soft before the other parts are hot enough to show the desired colors. The reheating is sometimes done over the fire, or on a plate laid over the fire.

Methods of Cooling.—The degree of hardness in a piece of carbon steel depends upon the rapidity of its cooling from the refining heat. Some tools, such as dies, files, etc., which must be extremely hard, are hardened by plunging them, when at the refining heat, into a bath of cold brine. The latter cools the steel faster than water, and leaves it much harder. Tools and articles such as springs, which require toughness rather than hardness, are cooled in oil. The oil does not cool them as rapidly as water.

Care should be taken not to remove the tools from the bath, when being hardened thruout, until they have completely cooled, as they are likely to crack.

Forging Heat of Tool Steel.—The temperature at which tool steel should be worked depends on the amount of forging and hammering to be done. If a large amount of hammering is necessary for shaping a piece, it should be worked at a yellow heat. At this heat the steel is plastic and works easily. Much heavy hammering is good for the steel, since it refines the grain. When the forging or tool is merely to be smoothed or finished, the work should be done at a temperature just above the refining heat.

Heating Steel for Hardening.—The fire used for heating

tool steel should have a good bed, or bottom, of hot coke, in order to heat the cold air coming thru the tuyere iron. If the air is not warmed very much and a piece in the fire is turned over occasionally, the heated portions of the piece will be cooled. This cooling will make it contract and tend to crack it. The piece should also be kept well covered with hot coke, in order that the oxygen in the air will not attack and decarbonize it.

Carbon steel should be heated slowly enough to obtain a uniform color on it. If it is heated too rapidly the corners and edges will become overheated before the main body of the piece has reached the proper temperature. Allowing these parts to cool to the proper temperature will not do much good, as the grain in them will be coarse and there will be internal stresses set up.

Importance of Uniform Heating.—If one part of a tool to be hardened is heated more than another there will be an unequal expansion. The contraction which takes place when the tool is cooled will also be unequal. This causes internal stresses in the tool, which may crack it at any time. For this reason pieces of tool steel sometimes break with a loud report after being hardened.

Hardening at a Rising Heat.—A piece of carbon steel should never be allowed to "soak" in the fire after having been uniformly heated to the desired temperature. This causes it to become decarbonized, coarse in grain, and brittle. It should be removed from the fire and hardened just as soon as the desired temperature has been reached.

Restoring the Grain.—In case the grain of a piece of steel has become coarse thru overheating, it may and should be refined in one of the following ways:

1. By reducing the size of the material with a trip-hammer or sledge, thereby closing the grain.

2. By allowing the steel to cool and then reheating it to the refining heat.

Restoring the grain by reheating may not make the steel quite as good as it was before being overheated. Unless it has been overheated for some time or actually burned, hammering will practically restore it to its original quality.

Caution.—If the refining heat of a piece of steel is 1400° F, and thru carelessness the piece is heated to 1600°, it should not be cooled in the air to 1400° and then hardened. This would give it the hardness of the 1400° temperature together with the coarse grain due to overheating. The grain of tool steel remains in the condition caused by the highest temperature to which it has been heated until it is cooled and reheated. It then adjusts itself to the new temperature.

Warping in Cooling.—When heated steel is cooled it contracts, and unless the contraction is uniform it is liable to be warped or bent out of shape. To avoid this warping as much as possible the piece must first be heated uniformly, and then cooled uniformly by dipping it in the cooling bath in the proper manner.

If, for instance, a carving knife were uniformly heated and dipped into oil or water so that one of the flat sides struck the bath first, that side would be cooled more quickly than the other and the blade would be badly warped. By dipping it in edge-wise both sides would be cooled at the same rate, and the warping would be very slight.

Cylindrical pieces are generally inserted end first in the cooling bath; while square flat pieces, carving knives, shear blades, and articles of similar character, are dipped edge-wise.

Hardening Thin Flat Articles.—Very thin flat pieces of steel are sometimes hardened by heating them uniformly to the refining heat and placing them between heavy plates of iron whose faces are smeared with oil. The insertion of the steel between the plates must be done as quickly as possible. This method leaves the steel hard, true, and flat.

Tempering Taps.—When hardening tools having teeth or

projections, such as taps and reamers, they should not be heated more than is absolutely necessary. The heating should be done in a muffle furnace, but in case this is not available it can be done over the forge fire by enclosing the tap in a piece of pipe, to prevent the teeth from coming in direct contact with the fire. In the latter method the pipe in which the heating is done should be longer and at least 2 inches larger in diameter than the tool. The tap must be heated slowly and revolved frequently, in order to obtain a uniform heat.

After the refining heat has been reached the tap is cooled in tepid water. It is plunged end first and then moved up, down, and around in the water, to cool it thoroly and to prevent the steam generated from retarding the cooling.

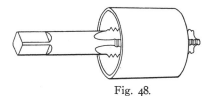

Fig. 48.

When the tap has been completely cooled it is taken out and polished with a special emery wheel, or with emery cloth, in order that the temper colors may be readily seen.

It is tempered by inserting in a heated collar, as shown in Fig. 48. It should be constantly revolved while inside the collar, and moved back and forth thru it, depending on how the colors are appearing. In no case should the teeth come in contact with the inside of the collar. When the desired color, deep straw or brown, has appeared, the tap is cooled in oil.

Tempering Carving Knives.—When hardening carving knives on a small scale they are generally heated in the same manner as a tap, *i. e.,* inside of a piece of pipe. The pipe should, however, be first heated uniformly by revolving it slowly in the fire. The knife is then held inside of it, and very little blast turned on. The heating should be done slowly, in order to avoid warping or bending. When heated uniformly to the refining heat, the blade is cooled in fish oil, dipping it edge-wise with the back of the knife down. If the blade becomes bent before hardening, no attempt should be made to straighten it below a red-heat, otherwise it will warp again when being cooled.

After the knife has been hardened it is polished on an emery buffer and held in the flame of the fire to temper it. The final cooling is done in oil, when the color of the scale is blue tinged with red.

Tempering Shear Blades.—In small shops shear blades are hardened in the following manner: Two wrought iron plates the same length as the blade, 1 inch narrower, and ⅝ inch thick are placed on either side of the blade, so that about 1 inch of the cutting edge is exposed for its entire length. Holes corresponding to those in the blade are drilled in the plates, and the three pieces are bolted together. They are then placed in a furnace, heated to the refining heat, and cooled in tepid water.

When the blade is cold the plates are removed, and one side of the blade polished, in order to watch the temper colors. The blade is tempered by standing it on edge lengthwise on a piece of hot iron. As soon as the desired color, a straw yellow, reaches the cutting edge, the blade is cooled in fish oil.

These plates prevent the body of the blade from becoming as hot as the cutting edge, and cause it to cool slowly. This makes the body tough for resisting shocks. The plates also keep the blade from warping when cooling.

Tempering Springs.—When pieces of steel must be toughened so that they will return to their original form when bent or twisted, they are generally "spring tempered." This is the same as ordinary tempering, except that more of the hardness is removed, making the steel tougher.

Fish or animal oil is generally used for cooling in spring tempering. It gives better control over the hardness, because the steel is not cooled quite so fast as in water. The latter can be used, but it makes it harder to properly gauge the tempering.

For many purposes a grade of steel made especially for springs gives better results than regular tool steel. It is therefore a good policy to state the requirements of a spring when ordering material for it.

Tempering springs on a small scale is generally done by the **blazing off** or **flashing process**. The spring is first hardened in the fish oil and then re-heated, while still wet with oil, in the flame of the fire. When the oil on it blazes up, it is plunged for an instant into the oil bath. This procedure is continued until the oil blazes uniformly over the entire spring at the same time, which is generally after about three plunges in the bath. It is then again completely cooled in the oil. Springs are seldom uniform in thickness, hence the thin parts heat more quickly than the others. The momentary plunge into the oil bath cools these thin parts somewhat without affecting the rest of the spring very much. In this way the entire spring is brought to the flash-point temperature of the oil, which is about 600° F.

When large numbers of springs are to be handled, an oil bath kept at the proper temperature is often provided for tempering. The springs are placed in this bath after being hardened, and are allowed to remain there for a certain length of time, depending upon their size. They are then removed and cooled in oil.

Case Hardening.—On account of the small amount of carbon in wrought iron and soft steel, they cannot be hardened to any appreciable extent. If, however, they are heated to a high temperature while in contact with some substance containing carbon, such as ground bone, charcoal, or charred leather, their outside surfaces will absorb some of the carbon. This gives these surfaces the characteristic properties of tool steel, so that they can be hardened and tempered in the same manner. The process of treating the iron or steel so as to make the outside surface hard is known as case-hardening.

A piece of material which has been case-hardened consists of a wrought iron or machine steel core with a tool steel surface. Machine steel is used ordinarily for case-hardening. Steel treated in this way is particularly valuable for bicycle parts, since it will not bend easily, resists shocks by reason of its soft core, and is much cheaper than tool steel. The depth to which the material is carbonized, or the penetration of the carbon, depends upon the temperature to which the material is heated while in contact with the carbonizer, the length of time it is maintained at that temperature, and the carbonizing substance used.

There are three practical shop methods which are used for case-hardening.

FIRST METHOD.—Small pieces and pieces which require only a very thin shell of hard steel are first heated to a high red heat, then removed from the fire and sprinkled with cyanide of potassium. The latter must be reasonably pure in order to obtain the best results. The pieces are reheated for a few seconds, to allow the carbon from the cyanide time to soak in, and are then quickly cooled in water. This method is also used when only the surface of a hole or a small part of a piece is to be hardened.

By taking a handful of sharp sand and scouring the piece under water while it is still hot, all of the dirt and scale may be removed.

SECOND METHOD.—It is often desired to give the surface of a tool a mottled effect when case-hardening it. This can be done in the following manner:

The tool is first polished and then placed in a cast iron pot containing molten cyanide of potassium. This pot is kept on the fire until after the tool is removed. The tool is allowed to remain in the cyanide until the desired absorption of carbon has been reached. Ten minutes is required for a penetration of about .001 inch. It is then removed with a pair of tongs and dropped thru a distance of 5 or 6 feet into cold water.

The same effect can be obtained by passing the piece thru a spray of water after its removal from the cyanide pot, and then cooling it. Wherever a fine spray strikes the piece a vine-like effect is produced.

Caution.—Do not dip wet tongs into molten cyanide, as this will cause the cyanide to spatter around. Cyanide crystals are deadly poison. Care should also be taken to avoid the fumes from the cyanide as much as possible, for they are very poisonous.

THIRD METHOD. **Pack Hardening.**—In most commercial practice case-hardening is done in the following manner:

The carbonizer, which may be ground bone, charcoal, or charred leather, is dried well and reduced to a fine powder. A layer of it about $1\frac{1}{2}$ inches thick is placed on the bottom of a hardening pot, and on top of it a layer of the articles to be hardened. These must not touch each other. Another layer of carbonizer is added, and on top of it another layer of the pieces. This building-up process is continued until the pot is full, when a final covering of carbonizer is added. A lid is put on, and all joints are closed with clay to prevent oxidation. The pot is then placed in a furnace and heated to a temperature of about 1800° F, a full orange heat.

When the carbonizing action has continued long enough, about six hours being required for a penetration of about $\frac{1}{16}$ inch, the pot is removed from the furnace and allowed to cool slowly. It is then opened, and the articles cleaned with a brush. They are reheated to a temperature of about 1450°, and quickly cooled in cold water or oil. This reheating refines the grain, making the final product tough and strong.

Hardening pots are made out of either cast iron or wrought iron. The latter stand the heat better and last longer, but are more expensive.

This process is sometimes employed to enrich the surface of low-grade tool steel. The tool steel is packed with a carbonizing material in iron boxes, and heated in a furnace. The contents of the box are kept at a temperature of about 1475° F for about two hours, depending upon the depth of carbonizing required. After removing the box from the furnace the pieces are withdrawn, and cooled in oil.

Treatment of High-Speed Steel.*

High-speed steel generally requires different treatment from high-carbon steel, on account of the peculiarities of some of its constituents. The same general method is usually followed, but slight modifications are sometimes required to obtain the best results. For this reason it is advisable to follow the special directions given by the manufacturer.

Cutting Stock.—High-speed steel should be heated for cutting, since breaking it cold has a tendency to produce cracks. Small stock is often cut by grinding a groove around it with an emery wheel and then breaking it.

Forging Heat.—The proper temperature for forging this steel is about 1800° F, a yellow heat. It should be heated slowly until it becomes red hot, and may then be heated faster up to a yellow heat. If heated too quickly the outside of the steel may become hot while the center is still comparatively cold. Hammering it in this condition is liable to cause internal cracks.

---

* For further information on the treatment of high-speed steel the student is referred to "On the Art of Cutting Metals," by Mr. F. W. Taylor.

The Fire used for heating high-speed steel should not be a freshly-made one. It should have burned for some time, in order to produce the intense heat necessary for proper hardening. There should be a good bed of hot coke around the steel, to bring it to the hardening heat quickly.

Heating for Hardening.—In heating the end of a high-speed steel tool for hardening it should be brought slowly to a full red heat, and then quickly heated to the melting point. While doing this the tool should be turned frequently, to insure a uniform high heat thruout the entire end. At this temperature the nose of the tool sweats or becomes wet. The higher the temperature to which the tool is heated for hardening the greater will be its property of red hardness, or the higher the temperature at which it will still hold its cutting edge.

Care should be taken when removing the tool from the fire to see that the point does not hit the coke. At this high temperature the steel is soft and crumbly, and will break easily. If the tool becomes pitted, or if some of the corners fall off due to the excessive heat, it will still be in good condition after grinding off the irregularities.

Cooling.—The tool is cooled from this high heat by any one of several methods. Its nose may be quickly cooled by the air-blast from an air compressor or power fan. Another way is to simply immerse it in oil. Cooling it in water tends to crack it; but tools are sometimes partially cooled in water and then finally cooled in oil. The latter method makes the tool somewhat harder than either air or oil cooling.

Lead Heat Treatment.—Still another method is to plunge the highly heated tool into a vat of molten lead at a temperature of about 1500° F. It is allowed to remain there for a time, depending on the size of the tool (ten minutes for an ordinary lathe tool), and is then transferred to another vat at a lower temperature. This method is not suitable for small shops, as it is more expensive than the air-blast or oil method.

Annealing.—High-speed steel sometimes becomes refractory when dressing it, so that it crumbles. In such cases it should be annealed. This may be done in the same manner that carbon tool steel is treated.

CHAPTER VII.

TOOL FORGING.

Selection of Steel for Tools.—There are so many grades of tool steel on the market that it is very hard to select the best material for a tool without knowing somewhat of the characteristics of each grade. This information is generally given in the catalogues of the manufacturers, which should be consulted before ordering the material. One of the best ways is to order the steel for a stated purpose, without specifying any particular brand, thus putting the responsibility of selecting the right kind on the manufacturer or his agent.

Steel is sometimes designated by the number of .01%'s of carbon that it contains. If there is 1% of carbon in it, it is known as 100 point carbon steel. Fifty carbon, or fifty-point carbon, indicates a steel containing .5% of carbon.

In order to provide a rough guide for the student and to illustrate the fact that different tools require different grades of steel, the following table is given:

% CARBON	USED FOR
.70 to .80	Blacksmiths' tools, such as rivet-sets, sledges, hand-hammers, fullers, flatters, etc.; wedges, pick-points, and other tools that are welded.
.80 to .90	Shear blades, caulking tools, punches for boilermakers, axes, rock drills, hand chisels, and drop-forging dies.
.90 to 1.00	Mining and rock drills, chisels, dies, shear blades, knives, and axes.
1.00 to 1.10	Lathe centers; small hand tools; knives, axes, and flat drills.
1.10 to 1.20	Lathe and planer tools, twist drills, reamers, milling cutters, granite cutters' tools, lathe centers.
1.20 to 1.30	Wood- and metal-turning tools, graving tools, etc.
1.30 to 1.40	Tools for turning chilled and hard metals; finishing tools, and cutters.

Before attempting to forge and harden his first tool a student should experiment with a sample of the tool steel, in order to determine its refining heat and to learn how to restore the grain if it is overheated. He should also practice drawing the colors on pieces of scrap machine steel.

Tool-steel stock should be cut while hot. If it is cut cold cracks are likely to be formed, which will appear when the tool is hardened.

Exercise 26.   Cold Chisel.   (Plate XXVII.)

STEP ONE.—Heat the head end to a yellow heat, and taper it as shown at 1.

STEP TWO.—Forge the other end to the form shown at 2 at a yellow heat. About $\frac{1}{4}$ inch of this end should extend over the sharp edge of the anvil, and the tapering should be continued up to that edge. The finishing may be done with a flatter at a temperature just above the refining heat. If it is hammered out with heavy blows when black, the grain will be crushed.

STEP THREE.—The extreme end, A, may be cut off with the hardie, or it may be cut partly thru and broken after the chisel has been hardened and tempered. The latter method exposes the grain and indicates whether the heat was correct. If the edge of the tool is too thin when cut it should not be upset, as this makes it likely to crack. It must be cut off shorter. The chisel should be allowed to cool slowly, in order to remove any internal stresses that may have been caused by improper hammering.

The cutting edge is tempered to a blue-tinged-with-red color, in the manner already described in the previous chapter. The tip is then ground on an emery wheel to an angle of 60°, as shown.

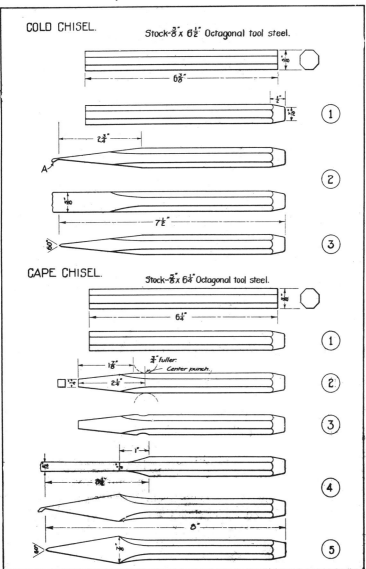

COLD CHISEL.

Stock–⅜" x 6½" Octagonal tool steel.

CAPE CHISEL.

Stock–⅝" x 6¼" Octagonal tool steel.

Test the chisel by chipping a piece of cast iron. If the cutting edge is too soft it should be rehardened at a higher temperature; while if it breaks, showing a coarse grain, it should be rehardened at a lower temperature.

Exercise 27.   Cape Chisel.   (Plate XXVII.)

The cape chisel, Fig. 49, is used for cutting grooves and for working at the bottom of narrow channels. The cutting edge, *A,* should be wider than the rest of the blade. The taper should extend to *B.* This permits the blade to "clear"

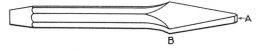

Fig. 49.   CAPE CHISEL.

the sides of a groove, or slot, when the groove is being cut to the width of the edge *A.*

STEP ONE.—Cut the stock to length, and taper the head end.

STEP TWO.—The other end is brought to a yellow heat, and tapered square, as shown at 2.

STEP THREE.—Make the fuller marks shown with ½- or ¾-inch top- and bottom-fullers. These marks should not be made too deep, or the blade will not be thick enough. Their object is to prevent the blade from being made too long.

STEP FOUR.—Place the end over the large part of the horn and flatten it with a hand-hammer in the manner shown at *A* in Fig. 50. Since the horn acts as a fuller, this stretches the stock lengthwise and enables one to make the end of the blade, *A,* in Fig. 49, wider than the section at *B* without making the nicks or sharp corners which would be formed if the edge of the anvil were used.

Extend the end *M* shown at *B* in Fig. 50 over the sharp

edge of the anvil, and finish the blade by turning it on edge and hammering it to a point. Smoothing may be done with a set-hammer and a flatter, as shown at *C* and *D* in Fig. 50.

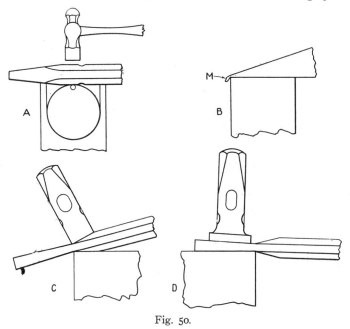

Fig. 50.

Harden and temper the cutting edge in the same manner as the flat chisel.

Exercise 28. Round-Nose Cape Chisel. (Plate XXVIII.)

The round-nose cape chisel is used for cutting oil grooves and for centering drills. In the latter capacity it is known as a centering chisel.

This chisel is made in the same manner as the cape chisel except that one edge of the blade is rounded, as shown at 5. This is done by placing the blade on a bottom-swage and using a hand-hammer or a flatter on the top edge.

Exercise 29.   Center-Punch.   (Plate XXVIII.)

The center-punch is so simple to make that no detailed description of the steps required is necessary. It is hardened in the same manner as the cold chisel, but is tempered to a brown or purple color. When tempered, the center-punch should mark tool steel without having its point dulled.

Lathe Tools.—In most machine-shop work high-speed steel tools are employed in preference to carbon tools, because they can be used for faster cutting and are more economical. For light lathe work, high-speed steel may be obtained in small pieces already hardened. Where a fine finish is desired and the cuts are light, carbon steel tools are used. They will take a keener edge than high-speed steel, but the cutting must be done more slowly. The following five exercises give the method of forming and tempering some of the common forms of high-carbon lathe tools.

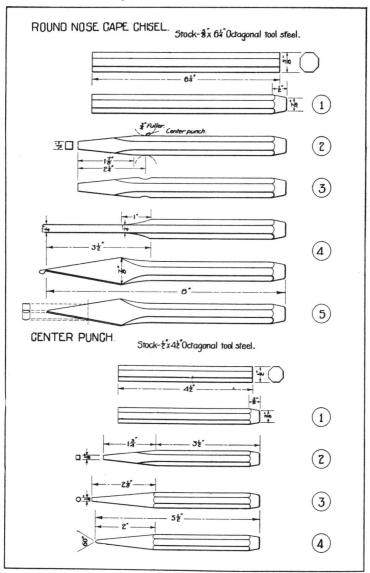

ROUND NOSE CAPE CHISEL. Stock-⅞″x 6¼″ Octagonal tool steel.

CENTER PUNCH. Stock-½″x 4½″ Octagonal tool steel.

Exercise 30. Round-Nose Tool. (Plate XXIX.)

STEP ONE.—Forge one end of the stock from three sides to a blunt point, as shown at 1.

STEP TWO.—Hammer out this end so that the top edge is thicker than the lower one and has clearance all around, as shown at 2. This is done because all the cutting done by this

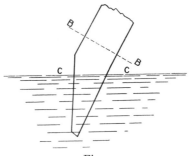

Fig. 51.

tool occurs at or near the tip. Trim off the end with a hot chisel, and bend it up slightly, as shown.

The hardening is done in the same manner as with the cold chisel. The nose should be heated up to the line BB in Fig. 51, and then cooled as far as CC. The final cooling is done when the temper color at the tip is light yellow.

Exercise 31. Cutting-Off Tool. (Plate XXIX.)

The cutting-off tool is used for making a narrow groove in work on a lathe. It is forged with the blade either on one side or in the center of the stock. The easier way is to have one side of the blade flush with the side of the tool, as in this exercise.

STEP ONE.—Cut the stock to length, and center-punch it, as shown at 1.

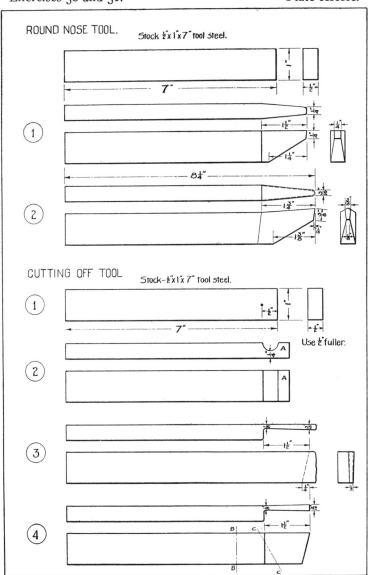

ROUND NOSE TOOL. Stock ½"x1"x7" tool steel.

CUTTING OFF TOOL Stock-½"x1"x7" tool steel.

Use ½" fuller.

STEP TWO.—Mark with a fuller, and draw out the part A either with a hand-hammer on the rounded edge of the anvil or with the trip-hammer. The hammering should be done with the fullered side down, in the same manner as the first step in forging flat-jawed tongs.

STEP THREE.—Taper the sides of the blade as shown at 3. Since the cutting edge of this tool is the extreme end, it must be made thicker than the rest of the blade, so that it will have clearance.

STEP FOUR.—Cut off the end of the blade with a hot chisel, making it appear as at 4.

In tempering this tool it is heated to the line BB and cooled to the line CC, in the same manner as the round-nose tool. The temper color should be light yellow.

Exercise 32.   Threading Tool.   (Plate XXX.)

STEP ONE.—Cut and mark the stock, as shown.

STEP TWO.—Fuller the end, as at 2.

STEP THREE.—Draw-out the blade with a set-hammer, a top-fuller, or under the trip-hammer.

STEP FOUR.—Cut off the end with a hot chisel. The cutting edge is generally ground by the person using the tool. Harden it in the same manner as the cold chisel, tempering it to a light straw color.

THREADING TOOL.   Stock–½″x1″x7″tool steel.

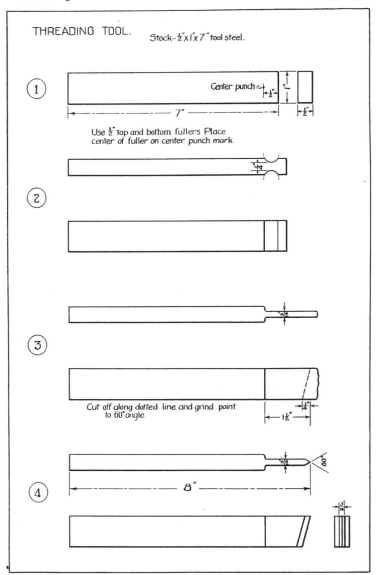

(1)

Center punch

1″

½″

7″

½″

Use ½″ top and bottom fullers Place
center of fuller on center punch mark.

¾″

(2)

(3)

3/8″

Cut off along dotted line and grind point
to 60° angle.

1¼″

1½″

(4)

3/8″

60°

8″

3/8″

Exercise 33. Side Tool. (Plate XXXI.)

Side tools, or side-finishing tools, are shaped as shown at 4. They are made with the blade at either the right or the left side, and are called right- or left-hand side-tools. The blades may be bent. Bent side-tools are forged in the same manner as the others, the blade being bent toward the shank afterwards.

STEP ONE.—Cut the stock to length, and mark it as shown.

STEP TWO.—Make a fuller mark as shown at 2, tipping the fuller so that the groove is cut deeper at one side.

STEP THREE.—Draw-out the end of the stock, C, at the rounded edge of the anvil with a heavy hand-hammer, the fullered side being down. Smooth it with a set-hammer. Trim the blade with a hot chisel along the dotted lines shown at 3.

STEP FOUR.—Finish the tool by giving the top edge of the blade the proper offset. To do this it should be placed with the flat side down over the rounded edge of the anvil, as shown in Fig. A. The shoulder of the blade should extend about $\frac{1}{8}$ inch beyond the outer edge. A set-hammer is placed on the blade close to the shoulder and given a few blows with a sledge, to produce the necessary offset.

In hardening this tool it should be placed in the fire with the cutting edge up, in order to avoid overheating. The blade is hardened by dipping it in water, as shown in Fig. B. Only the small corner of the blade D should be allowed to remain red-hot. The tool is removed from the water, quickly polished on the flat side of the blade, and tempered to a light yellow color. The entire cutting edge should be uniform in color. If this is not the case and it is blue at one end and straw at the other, the blue end has not been cooled enough. The tool should then be rehardened, this time tipping it so that the end of the blade which was too soft will be deeper in the water.

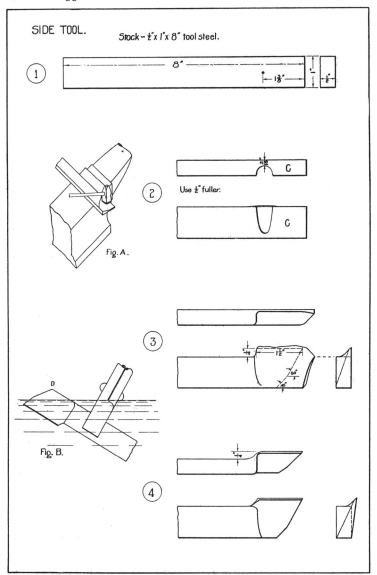

SIDE TOOL.   Stock – ½" x 1" x 8" tool steel.

1

8"

1⅜"   1"   ½"

Fig. A.

2

Use ½" fuller.

C

C

3

1½"

60°

Fig. B.

D

4

Exercise 34.   Boring Tool.   (Plate XXXII.)

STEP ONE.—Cut the stock to length, and mark it as shown.

STEP TWO.—Make a fuller mark as shown at 2.

STEP THREE.—Draw-out for the thin shank either under the trip-hammer or at the rounded edge of the anvil with a sledge or heavy hand-hammer. The length of this shank varies according to the depth of the hole in which the tool is to be used.

STEP FOUR.—Bend the nose as shown. Only the tip of this nose need be hardened and tempered. The temper color is the same as for the other lathe tools, *i. e.,* light yellow.

It is sometimes necessary to use a boring-tool for turning a recess having sharp corners. In this case the nose is hammered flat before bending, as shown in Fig. A. It is then bent up, as in Fig. B, and the cutting edge ground square.

Exercise 35.   Cross-Peen Hammer.   (Plate XXXIII.)

In forging the cross-peen hammer of this exercise two students should work together. The stock used should be 8¼ inches long, giving enough material for two. When only one hammer is required the stock should be long enough to work it without the use of tongs. With handle it should weigh about 2¾ lbs.

STEP ONE.—Mark the stock as shown at 1 with a chisel and a center-punch.

STEP TWO.—Bring the steel slowly to a yellow heat, and punch it with an eye-punch similar to the one shown in Fig. 52. The end of this punch is shaped somewhat like a dull center-punch, so that it can be easily driven thru the stock without cutting out too much material. The punch should be removed from the hole after each blow, in order to see if the hole is being punched straight. This also cools the punch, and

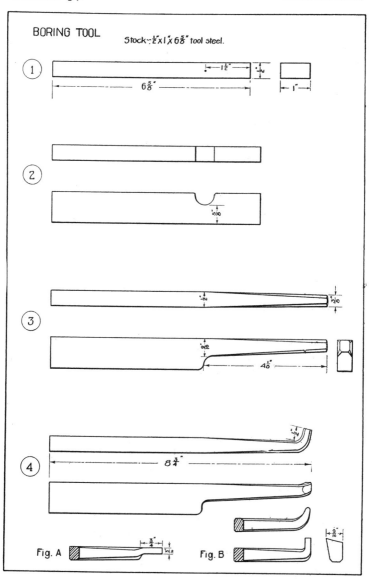

BORING TOOL   Stock-½″×1″×6⅝″ tool steel.

Fig. A   Fig. B

prevents it from bending. When the hole has been punched nearly thru from the one side, the punch should be removed and cooled. Punching is then finished from the other side.

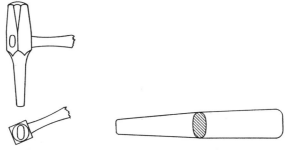

Fig. 52. EYE-PUNCH.   Fig. 53. DRIFT-PIN.

STEP THREE.—Drive a tool-steel drift-pin, Fig. 53, into the hole. The bulging sides of the piece should then be hammered down to the size of the bar with a sledge, and smoothed with a flatter. Always remove the drift-pin before reheating the piece.

STEP FOUR.—Draw-out the face end to the form shown.

STEP FIVE.—Trim the face with a hot chisel. Drive the drift-pin in from each side, making the shape of the eye as shown. Cut off the stock at the middle, and draw-out the peen end in the same manner as a hand chisel is forged, either under the trip-hammer or with a heavy hand-hammer. Finish it with a flatter.

STEP SIX.—Finish trimming both ends, making the hammer appear as at 6.

STEP SEVEN.—When cold grind the face and peen slightly convex, as shown.

For hardening, the entire hammer is slowly heated to the refining heat. In removing it from the fire, one jaw of a pair of tongs should be inserted in the eye. The face is hardened first by slowly inserting about 1½ inch of the end in water, as

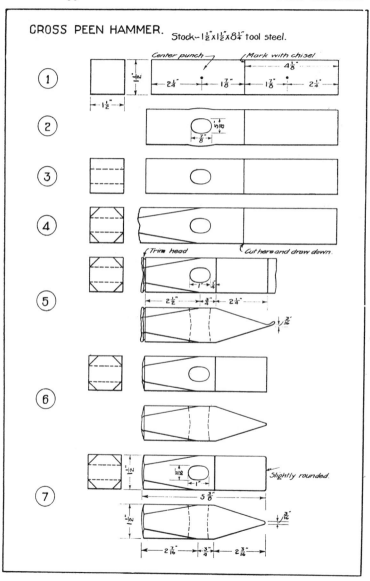

CROSS PEEN HAMMER. Stock—1½"×1½"×8¼" tool steel.

was done with the cold chisel. When it has cooled enough, the peen is hardened in the same manner, care being taken not to cool the stock around the eye. While cooling the peen, water should be allowed to drip on the center of the face. This prevents the colors from running down before the peen has been cooled enough, and insures a uniformly hardened face. If the face were cooled by merely dipping it in water, the outside edges would harden faster than the center and be more likely to crack.

After cooling, the ends are polished with an emery brick, the heat around the eye being held for tempering. Dark brown is a good temper color for the face, and brown or purple for the peen. If the desired color reaches the face first, the face should be placed in water until the proper color has reached the peen. The two ends are then dipped alternately in water. This allows the eye to cool slowly, making it tough.

Exercise 36. Small Cross-Peen Hammer. (Plate XXXIV.)

This hammer is forged and tempered in the same manner as the cross-peen hammer of Exercise 35. It should weigh when finished about $1\frac{1}{4}$ pounds.

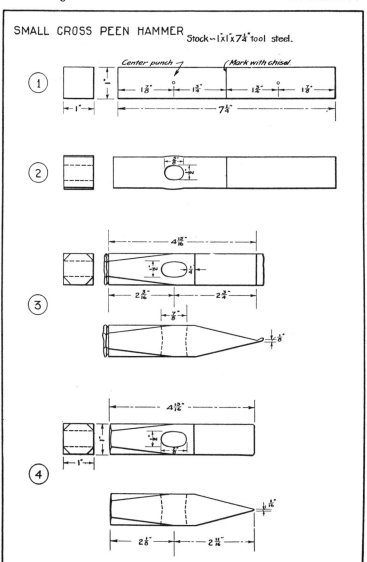

SMALL CROSS PEEN HAMMER Stock~1″x1″x7¼″ tool steel.

Exercise 37.   Ball-Peen Hammer.   (Plate XXXV.)

In making the 2-pound ball-peen hammer shown, a piece of 1½-inch square tool steel 6½ inches long is used.   This is enough stock for two hammers; if only one is wanted the stock should be long enough to work without using tongs.

STEP ONE.—Mark the stock as shown with a chisel and a center-punch.

STEP TWO.—Flatten out the end as shown at 2.   If this is done after punching the hole, the hole is likely to become too large.

STEP THREE.—Punch the hole in the same manner as in Exercise 35.   Drive in a drift-pin, and hammer down the sides as shown at *A* in Fig. 54 until they are straight.

STEP FOUR.—Roughly shape the hammer with top- and bottom-fullers, as shown at *B* in Fig. 54.

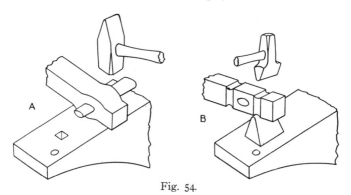

Fig. 54.

STEP FIVE.—Round the body of the hammer at the rounded edge of the anvil with a top-fuller and a set-hammer.   The body should taper in both directions, and be thicker at the center than at the edges.

STEP SIX.—Cut the stock at the chisel mark from four

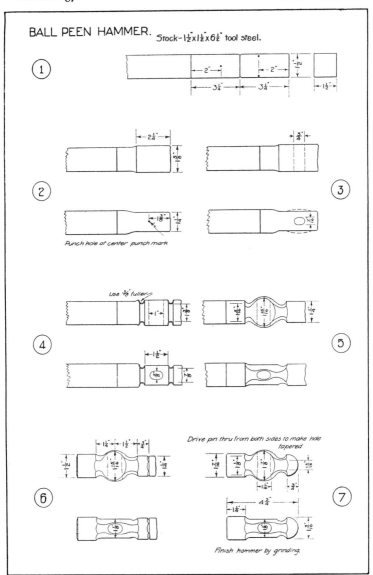

BALL PEEN HAMMER. Stock—1½"x1½"x6¼" tool steel.

Punch hole at center punch mark

Use ⅜" fuller

Drive pin thru from both sides to make hole tapered

Finish hammer by grinding.

sides, in order to insure a square end. Draw-out the face, swage it, and trim it with a hot chisel. The peen should then be cut to length, and the corners cut off. It is rounded in a bottom-swage. The reason for finishing the face before the peen is that it is hard to hold the peen with a pair of tongs.

Grind both ends, making the edges of the face slightly rounded, to prevent the hammer from marking hot material.

This hammer is hardened and tempered in the same manner as the cross-peen hammer.

Exercise 38.   Hot Eye-Chisel.   (Plate XXXVI.)

If only one hot chisel is necessary, it may be forged on the end of a bar long enough to handle easily; but if two are wanted, the stock should be cut 10 inches long.

STEP ONE.—Mark the stock as shown.

STEP TWO.—Punch the hole in the manner described in Exercise 35.

STEP THREE.—Draw-out the head either under the trip-hammer or with a sledge. Finish it with a flatter, and cut off the end with a hot eye-chisel. In trimming the end it should be made slightly convex.

STEP FOUR.—Make fuller marks, as shown at 4, with ⅝-inch top- and bottom-fullers. The stock should be turned over in doing this, to insure a uniform depth of the cuts.

Punch and draw-out the head for a chisel at the other end of the stock in the same manner. Cut the stock at the center from two sides only, in order to have the blades square across the ends when drawn-out.

STEP FIVE.—Draw-out the stock for the blade either under the trip-hammer or with a sledge, and smooth it with a flatter. When trimmed the blade is hardened and tempered to a blue color, in the same manner as the hand cold chisel of Exercise 26.

HOT EYE CHISEL. Stock— 1¼" x 1¼" x 10" tool steel.

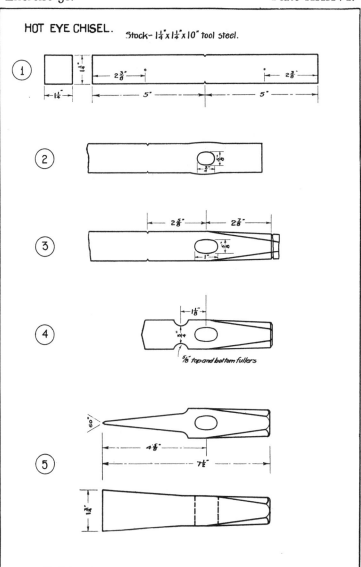

Exercise 39.   Cold Eye-Chisel.   (Plate XXXVII.)

For a cold chisel the stock is marked, the eye punched, and the head drawn-out and finished in the same way as for the hot chisel. After cutting the stock at the middle the blade is drawn-out, either under the trip-hammer or with a sledge. Care should be taken in doing this to keep the sides rounding, since a chisel of this form is much stronger than one with straight sides. This chisel is hardened like a hand chisel, and tempered to a brown or purple color. The edge should be ground slightly convex.

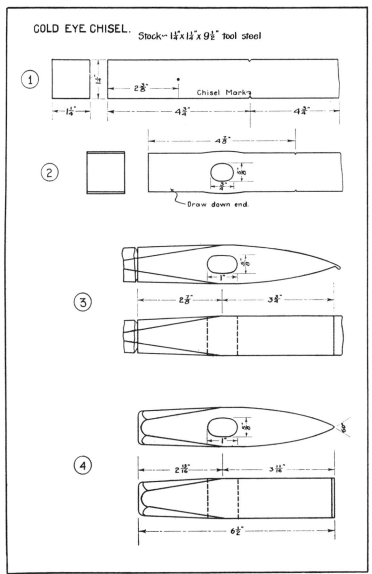

COLD EYE CHISEL. Stock~ 1¼"x 1¼"x 9½" tool steel

① 1¼"
2⅜" Chisel Marks
1¼" 4¾" 4¾"

② 4⅞"
5/16
¾"
Draw down end.

③ 5/16
1"
2⅞" 3¾"

④ 5/16
1" 60°
2 13/16" 3 11/16"
6½"

Exercise 40. Geologist's Pick. (Plate XXXVIII.)

This pick, which is intended for the use of students of geology, should weigh about $2\frac{1}{2}$ pounds when finished.

STEP ONE.—Mark the $1\frac{1}{4}$ x $1\frac{3}{4}$-inch stock with a center-punch and chisel, as shown.

STEP TWO.—Punch the hole for the eye.

STEP THREE.—Insert a drift-pin in the hole, and flatten the sides. With a hot chisel cut the stock part way thru at a distance of $\frac{3}{16}$ inch from the edge of the hole, on both sides of the eye. These cuts should be finished with a very thin fuller, or with a hot chisel having a rounded edge, in order to make the bottom of the cuts round, as shown at 3.

The material should then be cut along the lines MN and OP. The material cut out in this way might be drawn-out instead, but this would be difficult without a beveled set-hammer. Cutting it out is somewhat easier and quicker.

STEP FOUR.—Draw-out the end C under the trip-hammer to the size shown.

If only one pick is being made, it should be cut off of the bar at the chisel mark shown at 1 ; but if two are wanted, the second pick is started in the same manner before cutting. The end D is then drawn-out under the trip-hammer to the form shown at 5.

STEP FIVE.—Insert the drift-pin in the eye, and smooth the stock around it with a set-hammer, as shown in Fig. A. Finish the head with a set-hammer and flatter, and cut it to length with a hot chisel, trimming from four sides, to insure a square cut.

STEP SIX.—Finish the pointed end with a flatter, and cut it to length. The face and point are then ground, hardened, and tempered. The point is first treated in the same manner as the cold chisel, being tempered to a dark blue. The head is then heated for about 2 inches, and hardened in the same

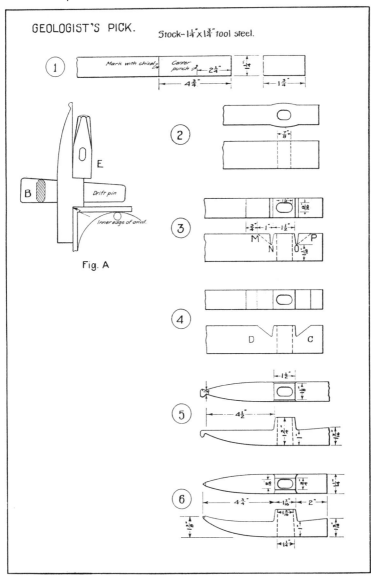

GEOLOGIST'S PICK.   Stock—1¼" x 1¾" tool steel.

Fig. A

manner. It is tempered to a brown or a dark straw color. In heating the head, care should be taken to prevent the heat from flowing back and softening the hardened point. This may be done by keeping damp coals around the point.

Exercise 41.   Hand Rock-Drill.   (Plate XXXIX.)

STEP ONE.—Cut a piece of $\frac{3}{4}$-inch octagon tool steel 16 inches long. Heat the end and draw it out, making it about $\frac{3}{16}$ inch thick, as shown at 1. The hammering should be done on two opposite sides, and the stock allowed to widen as much as possible.

STEP TWO.—Trim the end at an angle with a hot chisel, as shown.

STEP THREE.—Finish trimming the end with a similar cut, forming the cutting edge shown at 3.

STEP FOUR.—Sharpen the edge with a hand-hammer, holding the stock flat on the face of the anvil. The blows should come at an angle of 45°, to force the metal back; and the drill should be rotated about the cutting edge, in order to make it circular.

After sharpening the drill, it is brought to the refining heat and hardened in the same manner as a cold chisel. The temper color should be a dark straw.

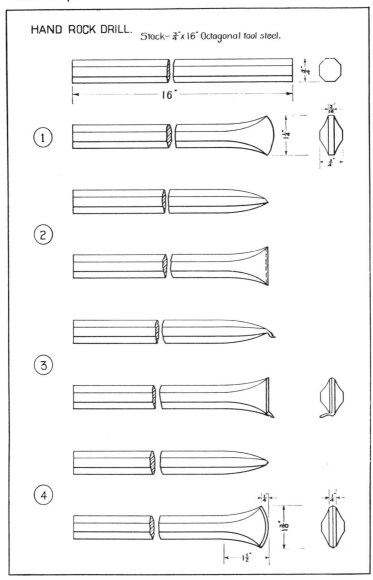

HAND ROCK DRILL. Stock~ ¾"x 16" Octagonal tool steel.

Exercise 42.   Machine Rock-Drill.   (Plate XXXX.)

STEP ONE.—Cut a piece of ¾-inch octagon tool steel 20 inches long.

STEP TWO.—Upset the end as shown at 2, and smooth it with a flatter.

STEP THREE.—Make small grooves along four sides as shown at 3 with a thin fuller, or with a hot chisel having a rounding cutting edge. These grooves extend back 2¼ inches, and are made for the purpose of guiding or holding the top and bottom V-fullers in place when fullering.

STEP FOUR.—Deepen the grooves with the top and bottom

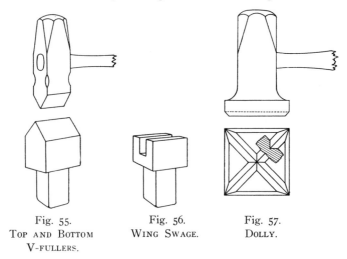

Fig. 55.
TOP AND BOTTOM
V-FULLERS.

Fig. 56.
WING SWAGE.

Fig. 57.
DOLLY.

V-fullers shown in Fig. 55. The stock should be turned during this operation, to insure uniformity in the depth of the fuller cuts.

STEP FIVE.—Make the sides, or wings, of the drill thinner and wider, using a bottom sow, or wing swage, Fig. 56, and

MACHINE ROCK DRILL. Stock– $\frac{3}{4}$″ x 20″ Octagonal tool steel.

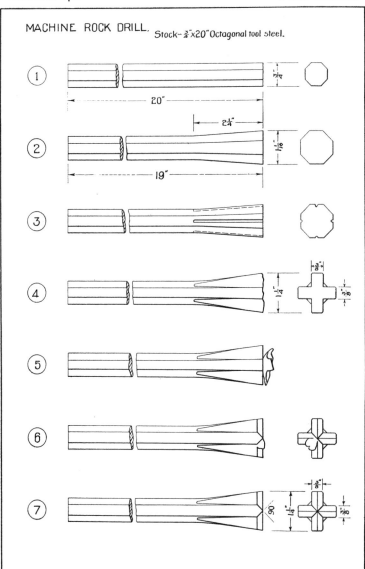

a square set-hammer. Trim off the end of the drill with a very thin hot chisel, making it square, as shown at 5.

STEP SIX.—Form the cutting edges, trimming the edges as shown at 6.

STEP SEVEN.—Finish the end with the dolly shown in Fig. 57. This dolly may be placed with its head resting on the anvil, the drill point being driven down into it while hot. Another method is to hold the drill across the face of the anvil with the dolly against the cutting end, and then strike the head of the dolly with a backing-hammer. If a very keen edge is desired on the drill, it should be filed while hot with a square file.

The hardening and tempering is done in the same manner as the cold chisel, the colors being drawn to a dark straw.

INDEX